Speaking for Themselves

Speaking for Themselves
Ethnographic Interviews with Adults with Learning Disabilities

Paul J. Gerber, Ph.D.
Fellow, International Academy for Research in Learning Disabilities
Professor of Special Education and Clinical Professor of Psychiatry,
Virginia Commonwealth University/Medical College of Virginia

and

Henry B. Reiff, Ph.D.
Assistant Professor of Education,
Coordinator of Graduate Programs in Special Education,
Western Maryland College

International Academy for Research in Learning Disabilities
Monograph Series, Number 9

Ann Arbor

THE UNIVERSITY OF MICHIGAN PRESS

Published in the United States of America by
The University of Michigan Press
Manufactured in the United States of America

1994   1993   1992   1991   4   3   2   1

Distributed in the United Kingdom and Europe by
Manchester University Press, Oxford Road,
Manchester M13 9PL, UK

Library of Congress Cataloging-in-Publication Data

Gerber, Paul J., 1950–
    Speaking for themselves : ethnographic interviews with adults with
learning disabilities / Paul J. Gerber and Henry B. Reiff.
       p.   cm. — (International Academy for Research in Learning
Disabilities monograph series ; no. 9)
    Includes bibliographical references and index.
    ISBN 0-472-10246-X (alk. paper)
    1. Learning disabled—Interviews. 2. Learning disabled—Case
studies. 3. Learning disabilities—Case studies.   I. Reiff, Henry
B., 1953– . II. Series.
LC4818.G47   1991
371.9—dc20   91-14615
                                            CIP

British Library Cataloguing in Publication Data
Gerber, Paul J.
  Speaking for themselves : ethnographic interviews with
adults with learning disabilities. — (International
Academy for Research in Learning Disabilities monograph
series, no. 9).
  1. Learning disordered adults
I. Title II. Reiff, Henry B. III. Series
362.3

ISBN 0-472-10246-X

This series of monographs published under the sponsorship of the International Academy for Research in Learning Disabilities is dedicated to the recognition of Professor Alexander Romanovich Luria, Ph.D., of the Union of Soviet Socialist Republics, a world-class professional whose work underscores a major development in an understanding of the neurophysiological development of children and adults with learning disabilities.

For our fathers Albert Gerber and Alvin I. Reiff

Acknowledgments

Much gratitude is expressed to Dean John S. Oehler of the School of Education at Virginia Commonwealth University for his support in the completion of this project. Thanks are also extended to Dr. William M. Cruickshank for his encouragement, to Dr. Rick Ginsberg and Patricia Popp for their comments and editing, and to Reginald Tinsley of Virginia Commonwealth University for typing the manuscript.

Contents

Abstract

Learning disabilities in adulthood have become an important agenda item for professionals, parents, and adults with learning disabilities themselves. In essence, the field has evolved from an emphasis on childhood, to adolescence, and on to the transition from high school to postsecondary education and societal systems and competitive employment. The experience of learning disabilities in adulthood is one that needs to be fully discovered and understood as the energies of the field evolve toward adult issues. Yet, available research has few answers, partly because a research framework has not emerged. In addition, few scientifically rigorous attempts have been undertaken to articulate the experience of adults with learning disabilities thus far.

What has not been sufficiently captialized upon in research efforts is that the experience of being an adult with learning disabilities can be conveyed via adults with learning disabilities themselves. Their perceptions about their lifespace, their unique perspective and retrospective cannot only be instructive but invaluable to all who seek to understand learning disabilities in adult development.

This research monograph uses an ethnographic methodology to allow adults with learning disabilities to speak for themselves. Nine adults with learning disabilities were studied regarding all areas of their personal and working lives. The areas addressed (by design of the authors) were educational issues, vocational issues, social and emotional functioning, and adjustment to daily living.

The nine adults, who ranged in age from twenty-two to fifty-six, were studied in three subcategories according to an index of educational and vocational achievement—high adjustment to adulthood, moderate adjustment to adulthood, and low (marginal) adjustment. All high-adjustment adults with learning disabilities attended college and received graduate and/or professional degrees. All moderately adjusted adults with learning disabilities graduated from high school and received some post-secondary training. None of the marginally adjusted subjects completed high school programs.

A wide variety of functioning was seen both within groups and between groups in the areas of inquiry. Degree of vocational success typically was a function of extent of education and in some cases related to severity of impairment. Subjects who had received advanced degrees were progressing successfully through their careers. Vocational success also characterized moderately adjusted subjects despite a string of different jobs and an unsystematic transition from school to employment. All marginally adjusted subjects were unemployed and had no near term or long-range plans for training or employment. Generally, theirs were lives of dependency, whether with parents or spouses. In the area of social and emotional functioning, the moderately adjusted group was qualitatively more proficient than the other two groups. All subjects seemed to be very cognizant of their struggles during childhood. They were aware of the residual effects of learning disabilities in adulthood. Adulthood was not the end of their struggle, however. In adult life the hurdles seemed to be as numerous but tened to be only as debilitating as the severity of their learning disabilities or the success of their systems of accommodation.

The interviews of the study's nine subjects demonstrate clearly that each day is one of trials and tribulations stemming from and related to learning disabilities. Poignant descriptions and quotations of the subjects' thoughts, feelings, and actions are highlighted through the ethnographic approach of the investigators. In each case, a view of adults with learning disabilities emerges that is most revealing and unique to the research literature.

Abstrakt

Lernschwierigkeiten im Erwachsenenalter sind zu einem wichtigen Punkt der Tagesordnung von Fachleuten, Eltern sowie lerngehemmten Erwachsenen geworden. Dieses Fachgebiet hat sich im besonderen aus der Wichtigkeit des Ubergangs von der Kindheit zur Jugend sowie von schulischen zu gesellschaftlichen Systemen und den Bedingungen eines im höchsten Grade wettbewerbsorientierten Arbeitsmarktes entwickelt. Die Beschaffenheit und das Erfahren von Lernschwierigkeiten im Erwachsenenalter verdienen gänzlich erforscht und verstanden zu werden, besonders in Bezug auf die Entwicklung des Forschungsgebietes hin zu Themen der Erwachsenenforschung. Die zur Zeit vorhandenen Forschungsergebnisse sind jedoch nicht sehr ergiebig, was zum Teil durch das Fehlen einer klaren Eingrenzung des Forschungsgebietes bedingt ist. Auch hat es bis zu diesem Zeitpunkt nur spärliche ernsthafte Versuche in der Wissenschaft gegeben, die Erfahrungen von Erwachsenen mit Lernschwierigkeiten zu erfassen und zu beschreiben. Ein Umstand, dem in der Forschung bisher nicht Rechnung getragen wurde, ist die Möglichkeit der Selbstdarstellung von Erwachsenen mit Lernschwierigkeiten. Ihre eigenen Aussagen über ihren Lebensraum, ihre besondere Perspektive und Retrospektive, können sich für alle an der Erforschung von Lernschwierigkeiten innerhalb der Erwachsenenentwicklung Interessierten nicht nur als nützlich, sondern geradezu als unschätzbar erweisen.

Die vorliegende Forschungsmonographie verwendet eine der Ethnographie zugehörige Methode, welche lerngehemmten Erwachsenen eine Möglichkeit zur Selbstdarstellung bietet. Neun lerngehemmte Erwachsene wurden sowohl in Hinsicht auf ihr Privat- als auch ihr Berufsleben untersucht. Die berücksichtigten (d.h. von den Forschenden dazu ausersehenen) Gebiete waren schulische und berufliche Fragen, soziales und emotionales Funktionieren, und Anpassung an die Erfordernisse des Alltags.

Die neun Erwachsenen, welche zwischen zwei und zwanzig

und sechs und fünfzig Jahre alt waren, wurden, je nach Zugehörigkeit zu bestimmten schulischen und beruflichen Errungenschaften—hoher Grad von Angepaßtheit an Erwachsenenalter, mäßige Angepaßtheit, und geringe (marginale) Angepaßtheit—in drei Untergruppen untersucht. Alle lerngehemmten Erwachsenen mit hoher Anpassung hatten eine Universität besucht und ein Studium absolviert. Alle mäßig angepaßten lerngehemmten Erwachsenen besaßen High School Abschluß und eine Form von weiterführender Bildung. Keiner der marginal angepaßten Erwachsenen hatte die High School abgeschlossen.

Sowohl innerhalb der Gruppen als auch zwischen den Gruppen konnte eine große Anzahl von verschiedenen Formen des Funktionierens im Rahmen des Untersuchungsgebietes festgestellt werden. Das Ausmaß des beruflichen Erfolges erwies sich durchwegs als eine Funktion von Tiefe und Ausmaß des Bildungsgrades. Die Untersuchten mit höherem akademischen Grad kamen erfolgreich in ihrer Karriere voran. Beruflicher Erfolg konnte auch als Trend in mäßig angepaßten Erwachsenen beobachtet werden, trotz einer Reihe von eingegangenen Arbeitsverhältnissen, charakteristisch für einen unsystematischen Übergang von Schule zu Berufsleben. Sämtliche marginal angepaßten Untersuchten verfügten weder über eine Arbeitsstelle, noch hatten sie Pläne bezüglich Ausbildung oder Anstellung in nächster oder fernerer Zukunft. Sie standen in einem Abhängigkeitsverhältnis zu Eltern oder Ehegatten. In Bezug auf soziales und emotionales Funktionieren erwies sich die Gruppe der mäßig Angepaßten als gewandter als die beiden anderen Gruppen. Alle Untersuchten schienen sich ihrer Probleme in der Kindheit und der anhaltenden Folgen von Lernschwierigkeiten im Erwachsenenalter bewußt zu sein. Erwachsenenalter bedeutete jedoch nicht das Ende ihres Ringens. Im Erwachsenenalter erschienen die Schwierigkeiten zwar genauso zahlreich zu sein, jedoch hing ihr negativer Effekt von Schwere der Lernhemmungen bzw. dem Erfolg ihrer Art von Anpassung ab.

Die Interviews mit den neun Erwachsenen der Untersuchung zeigen deutlich, daß sie von Tag zu Tag aufs Neue schmerzhaft versuchen müssen, gegen ihre Lernschwierigkeiten anzukämpfen. Ergreifende Beschreibungen und Zitate von Gedanken, Gefühlen, und Handlungen werden durch den ethnographischen

Ansatz der Untersuchenden zum Vorschein gebracht. In jedem einzelnen Fall kommt ein für die Forschung äußerst aufschlußreiches und einzigartiges Bild von lerngehemmten Erwachsenen zum Vorschein.

Résumé

On a étudié ces neuf adultes dont l'âge variait de vingt-deux à cinquante-six ans, dans trois sous-catégories selon un barème de réussite en éducation et dans la profession—adaptation supérieure à la vie adulte, adaptation modérée, et adaptation inférieure (marginale). Ceux qui furent classés dans la catégorie d'adaptation supérieure, avaient tous suivi des cours universitaires et reçu un diplôme soit universitaire soit professionnel. Ceux classés dans la catégorie modérée, avaient reçu un diplôme d'études secondaires et avaient poursuivi quelques cours supplémentaires. Aucun des marginaux n'avait fini l'école secondaire.

Une grande variété de fonctionnements furent remarqués dans les groupes et entre les groupes des catégories étudiées. Le degré de réussite professionnelle provenait typiquement de la longueur et de la qualité de l'éducation. Les sujets qui avaient reçu un diplôme d'études supérieures continuaient de progresser avec succès dans leur profession. La réussite professionnelle était aussi une tendance chez les adultes à adaptation modérée, malgré plusieurs changements d'emplois caractéristiques d'une transition peu systématique entre l'école et le travail. Tous les marginaux étaient sans emploi et n'avaient aucun projet de travail ou de formation professionnelle à long terme ou immédiat. En général, ils vivaient dans la dépendance de leurs parents ou époux. Dans le contexte du fonctionnement social ou émotionnel, les adaptés modérés étaient plus efficaces qualitativement que ceux des deux autres groupes. Tous les sujets semblaient se rendre compte des luttes qu'ils avaient eues pendant leur enfance. Ils se rendaient compte de l'effet résiduel de leur incapacité d'apprendre en tant qu'adultes. La lutte continuait dans leur vie d'aujourd'hui et les obstacles qui semblaient être aussi nombreux, tendaient à être aussi débilitants que la sévérité de leur incapacité ou que la réussite de leurs moyens d'adaptation.

Les entrevues des neuf adultes démontrent clairement que

chaque jour est un autre jour d'épreuves dues et liées à l'incapacité d'apprendre. Les descriptions poignantes, pensées, sen-
timents, et actions sont décrits dans le travail ethnographique
des chercheurs. Dans chaque cas, une image de cet adulte ressort,
image révélatrice et unique dans la littérature de recherche.

Sumario

La habilidad limitada de aprender de adultos se ha hecho un nuevo campo de investigación para los profesionales, para los padres, y para los afectados mismos. Esencialmente se ha evolucionado el campo de investigación desde un énfasis en la niñez hacia uno en la adolescencia, y de ahí a un enfoque en la transición de la escuela a tales sistemas sociales más competitivos como el empleo. La experiencia de tales inhabilidades entre las personas mayores es una que merece ser descubierta en más detalle, una que requiere una mejor comprensión a medida que el enfoque en este campo de investigación se evoluciona hacia asuntos que conciernen a los adultos. Pero la investigación ya realizada tiene pocas respuestas, en parte porque no ha surgido todavía ningún plan fijo de trabajo. Además de eso, hasta el momento se han ensayado pocas tenativas rigorosamente científicas para articular la experiencia del incapacitado mismo.

Lo que no se ha propuesto en el esfuerzo de hacer nuevas investigaciones es el que pueda ser comunicada por los afectados mismos las experiencia de ser un adulto que tiene dificultades con el proceso de aprender. La percepción que tienen ellos de su propio espacio vital, su perspectiva y su retrospectiva únicas, no sólo pueden ofrecernos unas lecciones provechosas pero también pueden ser de un valor inestimable para todos los que tratan de comprender la inhabilidad de aprender del individuo mayor.

El monógrafo presente emplea una metodología etnográfica que les permite la oportunidad de hablar por sí mismos a los mayores afectados con una incapacidad limitada de aprender. La vida particular y profesional de nueve adultos con dificultades definidas fue estudiada. Por decisión de los investigadores, el enfoque del estudio fueron tópicos relacionados con la educación, con el trabajo, con la interaccínn social y la vida emocional, y con la adaptación a las exigencias de la vida diaria.

Se estudiaron a nueve adultos entre las edades de veitidós y cincuenta y seis años que se subdividieron en tres categorías según un índice de éxito educacional y profesional—adaptación máxima, adaptación moderada, adaptación mínima o marginal a las exigencias de las vida adulta. Todos los adaptados máximos habían asistido a la universidad y habían recibido diplomas profesionales a veces otorgados por facultades de estudios para graduados. Además, todos los que se habían adaptado moderadamente se graduaron del colegio y habían recibido algún tipo de entrenamiento después de la segundaria. Ninguno de los menos adaptados habían terminado su programa de formación segundaria.

Se observó una gran variedad de adaptación y de habilidad tanto dentro de cada grupo como entre los varios grupos en las areas de investigación. Típicamente el nivel de éxico profesional fue una función de la profundidad y de la amplitud de los estudios académicos realizados por los sujetos. Los que habían recibido diplomas profesionales avanzados progresaban con éxito en sus carreras. Se observó que el éxito vocacional es una tendencia entre los sujetos adaptados medianamente a pesar de la serie irregular de oportunidades de empleo que tipifica una transición no sistemática de la escuela al empleo. Todos los adaptados marginalmente no tenían empleo; no habían formado planes para su entrenamiento ni para encontrar empleo sea a largo sea a corto plazo. Generalmente vivían dependientes de sus esposos o de sus padres. En cuanto a su adaptación emocional y social, los moderadamente adaptados eran cualitativamente más competentes que los otros dos grupos. Todos los sujetos parecían bien conscientes de sus luchas durante su niñez. Se daban cuenta clara de los efectos residuales de sus inhabilidades en sus años mayores. El ser individuo mayor no era el fin de su lucha diaria sin embargo. Durante sus años mayores los obstáculos parecían tan numerosos como antes, pero tendían a constituir debilidades no sólo como factor de la severidad de su inhabilidad sino también como resultado de su propio sistèma de adaptarse.

Las entrevistas de los nueve sujetos del estudio demuestran claramente que cada nuevo día es otro día de obstáculos y de luchas que tienen su origen y se relacionana a su inhabilidad de aprender. Se presentan unas descripciones muy afectivas y unos pensamientos agridulces además de sentimientos y acciones cordiales que se han subrayado por medio del método etnográfico de los investigadores. En cada caso surge una visión del adulto que tiene una habilidad limitada de aprender, una visión sumamente reveladora y única en la literatura de investigación actual.

CHAPTER 1

Review of the Literature

In recent years the field of learning disabilities has begun to focus its energies on adults with learning disabilities. Prior to this time, a school-age emphasis and academic skills orientation resulted in a lack of awareness about the adult population. However, beginning with the federal initiative of transition from school to work (Will 1984), the field began to divert its attention to the development of programs and services beyond the school-age years. Agencies such as the National Institute for Handicapped Research (now National Institute for Disability Research and Rehabilitation) (Gerber 1984) and the Rehabilitation Services Administration (Gerber 1981) have made noble efforts to address adult concerns, but those in the field have not yet determined the extent of services in adulthood. As awareness of adult concerns grows, policy makers and public consensus will direct future choices in terms of services for adults with learning disabilities.

A major concern about the direction of services and program development for adults with learning disabilities in this country stems from the paucity of research and less than adequate literature base on which to formulate decisions (Gerber 1985; Gerber and Mellard 1985). Interestingly, several European countries already have programs in place. Gerber (1985) provided cross-cultural studies of systems for this population in two countries, Denmark and the Netherlands. The studies found differing philosophies about programming for adults with learning disabilities. In the Netherlands, there was a drop in services at the adult level because learning disabilities were viewed as an edu-

The review of the literature was published in slightly different form in *Thalamus* 6, no. 1 (Spring, 1988); 1–32, under the title "Studies on Learning Disabled Adults: Methodological and Substantive Considerations." The third author of the paper was Dr. Rick Ginsberg, associate professor of educational leadership and policy at the University of South Carolina.

cational phenomenon. In Denmark, a well-established service delivery system for adults with learning disabilities had been in place for at least a decade. In the near future, the United States must make a decision about services for adults with learning disabilities (either the Dutch or the Danish model), but the decision should be based on what is known about the learning disabled adult experience. A close examination of the existing data in the American literature may point the way to more effective and valid approaches to meeting the needs of adults with learning disabilities.

Currently, researchers in the field tend to develop conclusions and constructs from traditional educational and psychological models that view adults with learning disabilities from "outside-in." That is, the focus of research has concentrated on conventional quantitative follow-up and longitudinal studies containing research questions from the researcher's perspective and bias. Instruments and statistical techniques vary from researcher to researcher. As a result, the current knowledge is quite uncertain. On the other hand, an "inside-out" research perspective may be more appropriate, since it would require a more qualitative approach where the individual subjects would describe various systemic components of learning disabilities in adulthood. Given the current limited understanding in this area, a qualitative "inside-out" approach is a logical direction for future studies of adults with learning disabilities.

The use of qualitative techniques in educational research mushroomed in the past two decades. Nevertheless, in special education, the use of such techniques is still in its infancy. In recent years, many researchers turned to expanding the methodological literature in this developing field. Notably, work by Lincoln and Guba (1985), Miles and Huberman (1984), Goertz and LeCompte (1984), Spindler (1982), and others that discussed improving qualitative techniques has added dramatically to the naturalistic paradigm (Lincoln and Guba 1985). What we refer to as the "inside-out" approach is assisting researchers in exploring areas previously only poorly understood. As Miles and Huberman (1984) explain, qualitative data are especially useful for inquiries in poorly charted waters:

Qualitative data are attractive. They are a source of well-grounded, rich descriptions and explanations of processes in local contexts. With qualitative data one can preserve chronological flow, assess local causality, and derive fruitful explanations. Then, too, qualitative data are more likely to lead to serendipitous findings and to new theoretical integrations; they help researchers go beyond initial preconceptions and frameworks. (15)

A review of past studies of adults with learning disabilities may demonstrate the need for a broadened methodological perspective in studying this population. The authors will highlight some of the strengths and weaknesses of the existing literature and show where and how future studies should direct themselves in order to illuminate issues for policymakers to consider in devising programs for adults with learning disabilities.

Literature on Adults with Learning Disabilities

In reviewing longitudinal and follow-up studies that focus on adult functioning, the authors necessarily exclude studies that followed up adolescents with learning disabilities while they were in school. Adolescent outcome studies are discussed only if they deal with teenagers who have exited from the school system. The review of the literature divides the studies into those conducted with individuals who had attended school before the passage of United States federal law P.L. 94–142 (The Education for All Handicapped Children's Act) and those that followed up adolescents and adults who had been in school after P.L. 94–142 became law. This categorization is required because of the presumable difference in services to individuals with learning disabilities in the pre- and post-P.L. 94–142 eras.

Pre-P.L. 94–142 Studies

Pre-P.L. 94–142 studies of adults with learning disabilities have been questioned because of a problem with identifying and selecting "legitimate" subjects with learning disabilities. The subjects of some adult studies went to school before many of the terms used to describe learning disabilities were common. As a result, early investigations tended to focus on individuals whose learning handicaps had been severe enough to receive attention in the "prelearning disabilities" era. The characteristics of these handicaps would most likely be subsumed by the classification of learning disabled or mildly handicapped today.

One of the earliest efforts to assess a learning handicap throughout the life span comes from the work of Menkes, Rowe, and Menkes (1967). In this study, the investigators conducted a psychological and social assessment of fourteen adults who were patients at a child psychiatric clinic from 1937 to 1946. A retrospective analysis of their records indicated that these individuals had been hyperactive and evidenced some kind of minimal brain dysfunction reflective of learning disabilities. The researchers found that neurological symptoms persisted into adulthood. Perhaps the most significant finding was that IQ was related to independent living skills and overall socioeconomic status. Since more severe learning disabilities may have a tendency to lower verbal or performance IQ scores either individually or in combination, this study indicates, at least implicitly, that the severity of the learning disabilities affects adult adjustment.

Most other adult studies report the persistence of some form of the disabling condition into adult life. Balow and Bloomquist (1965) discovered with thirty-two former reading clinic clients that reading disabilities continued to affect these individuals as adults and that remediation had not seemed particularly helpful. Additionally, these adults suffered from an unusual degree of emotional and social adjustment difficulties. Hardy (1968) reported similar results with forty former reading handicapped adults who were compared to a control group of normal adult readers. Again, in spite of academic gains, reading continued to pose significant problems and social adjustment was inadequate. However, neither of these studies commented on a relationship that appears more than coincidental: adults whose school remediation was unsatisfactory seemed to have a high degree of social and emotional adjustment difficulties.

Silver and Hagin (1964) carried out a landmark study whose

methodology served as an impetus for other studies of adults with learning disabilities. This study investigated twenty-four former reading clinic clients by examining the relationship of an extensive battery of psychoeducational tests from school years to specific measures of adult adjustment. The researchers found that neuropsychological problems in spatial and temporal organization persisted into adult life. These particular characteristics have been observed repeatedly in both children and adults with learning disabilities. This report also reiterated that the severity of the learning disabilities correlated with overall adult adjustment.

The Silver and Hagin study acted as a model for probably the best-known follow-up study of adults with learning disabilities. Rogan (Lehtinen) and Hartman (1976) adopted the methodology of comparing extensive school records to indicators of adult adjustment. They examined ninety-one adults, all of whom had been labeled learning disabled and attended the Cove School in Evanston, Illinois. While the findings were somewhat mixed, certain general patterns emerged. The dominant concern of most of the respondents was a lack of adequate social and personal relationships. Vocational problems seemed related more to social inadequacies than to vocational incompetence per se.

The Rogan and Hartman report also documented that a significant number of their adult subjects with learning disabilities had achieved a surprisingly high degree of adjustment. Three variables may have played a significant role. First, those individuals who reported the greatest degree of satisfactory adult adjustment tended to have been less severely learning disabled than those who had difficulty with adult life. Second, the overall program at the Cove School provided exactly the type of services and support to enable individuals with learning disabilities to achieve a maximum amount of autonomy. Finally, most of the students at the Cove School came from relatively affluent families in which the need to provide special considerations for children with learning disabilities had already been recognized. Other studies generally had disclaimed the effectiveness of remediation efforts. The Rogan and Hartman study implies that a program geared directly toward the needs of students with learning disabilities can have a positive impact, at least on individuals with mild to moderate learning disabilities who come from stable, affluent, and supportive home environments.

Rawson (1968) also provided evidence that a successful school experience combined with other favorable circumstances may be a common feature in successful adults with learning disabilities. This study followed up fifty-six adults who had been students in a special private school. Rawson reported that these adults had occupations in the upper socioeconomic level and had made adequate social adjustment. These findings become more meaningful when the background of these individuals is considered. They came predominantly from affluent families, tended to have high IQs, and were less severely learning disabled than the individuals in most of the other studies.

The work of Abbott and Frank (1975) also challenged studies that reported limited efficacy of remediation. This study investigated the school careers and general adolescent adjustment of 139 students who had been enrolled at the Pathway School in Audubon, Pennsylvania, between 1962 and 1971. Data took the form of parents' responses to a questionnaire or phone interview. Although the results were mixed, many parents reported that they were satisfied with the school program and that their children had made successful adjustments to adult life. As much as these responses are encouraging, the use of secondary sources (i.e., parents), the subjective nature of the questionnaire, and the predominantly upper middle-class background of the respondents limit the generalizability of the findings.

In 1985, Silver and Hagin published additional results from their research conducted prior to P.L. 94–142. This study presented a dramatic example of how different backgrounds determine different prognoses for adult adjustment. In their 1964 study, they noted the persistence of disabilities into adult life for a sample that came from the Bellevue Hospital Clinic population, the poorest of the Lower East Side of New York City. The study published in 1985 drew on subjects from relatively affluent families who had placed their children in private practice. As adults, these individuals evidenced an overall successful adaptation. Silver and Hagin suggested that the prognosis for adult adjustment of individuals with learning disabilities can be

favorable if appropriate educational interventions and environ-
mental support exist.

The general characteristics of adults with learning disabilities
that emerge from most pre–P.L. 94–142 studies are captured in
an attempt by Buchanan and Wolf (1986) to profile adults with
learning disabilities. This quantitative study with clinical interpretations investigated the lives of thirty-three adults who had
attended school before P.L. 94–142 had taken effect. Personal
histories and records indicated that most of these adults characterized their school experience as negative. In order to provide
a quantitative as well as qualitative psychoeducational profile,
the researchers administered to the subjects the Wechsler Adult
Intelligence Scale Revised (WAIS-R), the Woodcock-Johnson
Psycho-Educational Battery (W-J), and a writing sample. Because the cognitive and academic-skill profiles of these adults
were strikingly similar to their profiles as children, the researchers
reached the same conclusion found in most longitudinal studies—
learning disability characteristics of childhood persist.

These results are in agreement with those of Frauenheim's
study (1978) of adults with learning problems who had attended
school in the pre–P.L. 94–142 era. Forty adult males who were
diagnosed dyslexic in childhood scored significantly below the
norm on reading, spelling, and math achievement tests. Not only
were severe residual learning problems present, but the current
learning difficulties were identical to those diagnosed in school.
Obviously, these findings do not attest to the adequacy of whatever specialized instruction these individuals may have received.
Frauenheim and Heckerl (1983) reconfirmed these conclusions
in a follow-up of eleven men from the 1978 study. This report
posited that the basic learning difficulties of childhood would
at least be evident in test performance patterns:

> Patterns of skill weakness and cognitive abilities, as measured
> by academic and psychological tests, have remained remark-
> ably consistent over a period of approximately 17 years . . .
> There seems to be only a limited awareness or acceptance
> that some learning disabled individuals may not achieve func-

tional literacy skills despite adequate intelligence and educational opportunities. (p. 345)

Summary of Pre-P.L. 94–142 Studies

Several themes emerge to explain both the differences and similarities in these studies. Most of the differences result from
methodological inconsistencies from one study to the next. The
populations differed significantly; characteristics were assessed
on a wide variety of measures; the focus of the investigations
ranged from quantitative measures of academic ability to largely
subjective personal reports of emotional adjustment.

Nevertheless, certain consistencies can be gleaned from this
body of research. The inadequacy of remediation attempts and
the negative school experience of many might be related to the
pre-P.L. 94–142 level of special educational services. The few
investigators who held a positive opinion about education efforts
examined private school programs that perhaps offered a more
effective experience than the pre-P.L. 94–142 public education
system. In addition, the majority of students in private programs
came from family backgrounds that at a minimum provided a
greater degree of support and services.

Even the most encouraging reports on adult adaptation recognized that learning disabilities persisted in at least some form.
The consistency of this finding argues that learning disabilities
represent more of a developmental deficit than simply a developmental lag or delay. Since specific academic disabilities seem
to persist, it would be expected that the most successful adults
with learning disabilities found vocational opportunities that did
not place great emphasis on skills in which they were deficient.
Rich descriptions, which are the hallmark of qualitative research,
can help to describe exactly how adults with learning disabilities
adapt to the demands of adult life and successfully conform and
cope with the reality of their personal deficits.

Post-P.L. 94–142 Studies

For the most part, pre-P.L. 94–142 studies focused on characteristics of adults directly related to learning skills. Few of the

studies detailed the types of situations where these deficits would be problematic for adults. Certainly, academic concerns assume less importance in most adult lives. Consequently, it seems more appropriate to examine how persistent learning disabilities affect more relevant aspects of adult life, namely, vocational and social adjustment. Studies of the last ten years have placed greater emphasis on these concerns.

Fafard and Haubrich (1981) interviewed twenty-one young adults who had received services for learning disabilities after the enactment of P.L. 94–142. As students, they required additional services throughout their school experience. Fafard and Haubrich concluded that although many of these young adults were in need of some kind of vocational assistance, vocational training was almost nonexistent in their school programs. The researchers also hypothesized that these individuals depended on organized structures for social activities. As a result, they often depended on family support for social activities.

White, et al. (1982) compared forty-seven young adults who had been diagnosed as having learning disabilities in school to fifty-nine non-learning-disabled young adults. They postulated five variables that distinguished adults with learning disabilities from non-learning-disabled adults: (1) satisfaction with employment (adults with learning disabilities had lower mean job status); (2) degree of involvement in social organizations; (3) involvement in recreational activities; (4) use of prescribed drugs; and (5) unformulated plans for future education. The researchers suggested that schools must prepare students with learning disabilities for adult adjustment.

Goyette and Nardini (1985) conducted a study that focused exclusively on vocational outcomes for young adults with learning disabilities. This study examined five hundred high school graduates with and without learning disabilities who were monitored for three years after graduation. The researchers expected that the individuals with learning disabilities would have more trouble finding and keeping work. While this result was confirmed, the researchers were struck more by the variability within the group with learning disabilities. Thus, research techniques that present truly individual portraits may best illuminate the meaning of these heterogeneous differences.

Summary of Post–P.L. 94–142 Studies

Taken as a whole, these studies do not paint an encouraging picture of the effects of P.L. 94–142. These quantitative studies do not provide any assurance that the post–P.L. 94–142 era is really different from the pre–P.L. 94–142 era. Furthermore, the paucity of research from the post–P.L. 94–142 era presents difficulties in ascertaining a consensus regarding what needs to be studied. Each of three reviewed studies has a different focus.

A unifying theme may develop from the implication that adults with learning disabilities are themselves in need of special services. The contemporary literature reinforces recent efforts to expand the age parameters for receiving services stemming from P.L. 94–142. Again, in order to ascertain the direction for future research, it will be essential to discover how and why individual adults with learning disabilities have succeeded or failed. Services promoting successful adult adaptation will be feasible when adults with learning disabilities clarify what has worked for them.

Taking Aim at the Future

Problems with population selection, the heterogeneous characteristics of persons with learning disabilities, demographic variables, attrition, differing outcome measures, lack of control groups, and different ages at follow-up have limited comparisons and interpretations of most longitudinal and follow-up studies of adolescents and adults with learning disabilities (Horn, O'Donnell, and Vitulano 1983). Nevertheless, several distinct trends appear from the studies that have been reviewed. Severity, persistence, and the possibility of successful adult outcomes are three distinct issues that these studies have addressed. Other reviews of studies of adults with learning disabilities (c.f., Spreen 1988) have delineated similar trends.

Severity. Certainly, it is not surprising that the severity of the learning disabilities seems to be a significant variable for the prognosis of learning disabled adult outcomes. A number of studies from the 1960s and early 1970s followed up adolescents

who had been identified previously as educationally handicapped. Since these studies focused on school outcomes of adolescents, and did not focus only on adulthood, the authors did
not include them in the review of the literature. Nevertheless,
their findings are relevant to and consistent with the adult outcome literature. For example, Huessy and Cohen (1976), Hunter
and Lewis (1973), and Weiss, et al. (1971) all reported that
severity plays the major role not only in determining the effectiveness of remediation in adolescents but possibly in predicting
adult adjustment. Similarly, Silver and Hagin (1964) and
Menkes, Rowe, and Menkes (1967) concluded that the severity
of involvement figures into overall adult functioning, especially
in the degree of independent living. Children with severe learning
disabilities tend to become adults with severe learning disabilities
who very often cannot overcome the obstacles of their
impairment.

The few clinical studies focusing directly on adults with learning disabilities corroborate quantitative findings, yet the qualitative information often proves the most interesting and perhaps
the most enlightening. For example, although Blalock (1981)
provided useful information about adults with learning disabilities in terms of group scores on psychoeducational measures,
the clinical profiles and anecdotes contribute more to a realization of what life is like for adults with learning disabilities.
Although such anecdotal accounts were not the main focus of
the study, they provide insight not usually obtained from strictly
quantitative data.

Persistence. Almost every cited study reviewed here confirms
the persistence of learning disabilities. The data from school
outcome studies of adolescents with learning disabilities also
attest to the persistent effects of learning disabilities from elementary school through high school (Fitzsimmons et al. 1969;
Hinton and Knights 1971). In the studies on adults that have
been reviewed, persistence takes the form of continued reading
difficulties (Balow and Bloomquist 1965; Frauenheim 1978;
Frauenheim and Heckerl 1983; Hardy 1968), unchanging and
depressed academic and cognitive profiles (Buchanan and Wolf
1986) and neurological symptoms (Menkes, Rowe, and Menkes

1967; Silver and Hagin 1964). A remaining challenge for researchers is to determine the extent of the functional limitations associated with these persistent learning disabilities.

What is lacking in this information is a sense of how these disabilities affect adult functioning. For example, Silver and Hagin (1964) referred to persistent problems with spatial and temporal orientation, but what exactly do these problems mean to adults with learning disabilities? Part of this answer may be found in the sort of clinical work with adults with learning disabilities described by Blalock (1981). Blalock described clients with learning disbilities who repeatedly became lost when they came for appointments. They were often late, and perhaps as a result, tended to be agitated and uncomfortable. This sort of description begins to detail what learning disabilities may mean in everyday life.

Another problem in understanding the persistence of learning disabilities is the pluralistic nature of the population. Goyette and Nardini (1985) found the heterogeneity of their sample of adults with learning disabilities to be the most salient characteristic. Again, variability becomes much more meaningful when examples of that variability are concrete. One of the cited studies (Buchanan and Wolf 1986) offers such concrete information by providing individual vignettes of some of the adults in the study. This method highlights individual differences, yet even this more clinical approach has some commonalities. For example, many of Buchanan and Wolf's (1986) sample had a limited understanding of how learning disabilities affected their lives as adults. Alternative methods of study are needed to identify variables lying beneath the surface of such observations.

Success Potential. The impact of the social ecology is highlighted by the studies detailing positive adult outcomes (Abbott and Frank 1975; Rawson 1968; Rogan and Hartman 1976; Silver and Hagin 1985). From these studies, the profile that emerges of the successful adult with learning disabilities reflects a moderate to mild impairment, a relatively affluent family background, and a positive educational experience. An unanswered question involves the interaction between the two latter variables. Does affluence simply allow an individual to take advantage of better educational opportunities, or do these families themselves provide a supportive environment that can facilitate adult adjustment?

Finally, although the post–P.L. 94–142 studies have several implications, the most salient may be the continuing dissatisfaction with the focus of education with regard to adolescents with learning disabilities. The recurring social and vocational difficulties of adults with learning disabilities illustrate that education has not met the needs of this population.

Conclusions

The available literature of longitudinal and follow-up studies suggests that learning disabilities are lifelong conditions that have various manifestations in the adult years. Academic issues become less important, mainly because their relevance to daily functioning diminishes in adulthood. Conversely, vocational and social issues assume greater import. But the majority of existing studies leave so many questions unanswered that planning for services is quite difficult.

Qualitative research—whether conducted through interviews, observation, or content analysis of written accounts—allows adults with learning disabilities to tell researchers what issues are truly important and relevant. Perhaps the greatest shortcoming of quantitatively oriented studies is that most do not really show how learning disabilities affect adults in personal terms. An especially perplexing issue is the distinction between the cumulative effects of a personal history of learning disabilities and the daily impact of specific deficits in perceptual and cognitive functioning. A need exists for more detailed and subjective information to help us discover what it is to be an adult with learning disabilities.

The present state of understanding of the adult population with learning disabilities is still woefully inadequate. The field will ultimately mature when it analyzes quantitative information from large studies of adults with learning disabilities that is guided by qualitative insights based on the thoughts and feelings of adults with learning disabilities themselves. In this way, quantitative and qualitative approaches complement each other and provide a synthesis of knowledge traditionally found in two opposing camps.

Responding to the Need for Research about Adults with Learning Disabilities

The data collected and reported in this monograph are in response to the many gaps of knowledge in the research literature on adults with learning disabilities. While the available research answers some questions and points toward areas for further inquiry, oftentimes it has raised more questions than it has answered. Research studies have created new knowledge, but application of that knowledge at this time may be premature and in some cases unwarranted.

Much existing research relying on quantitative methodologies is based on preconceived notions or assumptions. Whether closed or open formats are used, these preconceptions inherently bias respondents' answers. In most cases, research designs have been based on traditional learning disabilities thinking—top heavy with a childhood/adolescence research base. The perspective of adulthood as a developmental stage, with its many acknowledged phases, may necessitate new conceptualizations beyond what is known from previous levels of development.

The commonsense approach to gathering basic research data on adults with learning disabilities favors a qualitative technique where adults with learning disabilities have an opportunity to speak for themselves. This enables a more clinically oriented methodology with the greater possibility of discovering nuances of behavior, degrees of severity, impact of limitations in functioning (either specifically or globally), ingredients for successful adjustment and adaptation, and a whole host of data that is of utmost value to professionals, parents, service providers, and adults with learning disabilities themselves.

CHAPTER 2

Methodology

Subject Selection

Nominations for subjects were solicited from learning disabilities advocacy groups, learning disabilities educators, allied health professionals, and university personnel. The nine subjects selected for the study are all bona fide persons with learning disabilities. Seven of the subjects were formally diagnosed as learning disabled by qualified psychologists and psychoeducational diagnosticians consistent with the state of the art practices of the field at the time of diagnosis. The remaining two had significant learning problems and received intensive tutorial help during their school-age years. Because they were not formally diagnosed in their school-age years, they were administered an adult learning disabilities screening instrument currently being used in a nationally recognized study (Gerber, Ginsberg, and Reiff 1990). Results of these screenings indicated that these two subjects could be classified as learning disabled with reasonable assurance.[1]

The subjects ranged in age from twenty-two to fifty-six years. All of the subjects were currently living in the greater New Orleans area and most were native Louisianians. Four of the nine subjects attended either school-age or postsecondary education programs outside the state of Louisiana.

The nine subjects were clustered into three categories according to their adjustment to adulthood: Subgroup 1: highly adapted to adult life; Subgroup 2: adapted to adult life; and Subgroup 3: marginally adapted to adult life.

Subjects were grouped according to their level of adaptability (i.e., high, moderate, low) on two categories of functioning: (1)

---

1. S1 showed a profile of difficulty in reading, spelling, impulsivity, and distractibility. S2's profile included difficulties with reading, spelling, writing, perceptual processing, impulsivity, and distractibility.

TABLE 1.   Subgroup Assignments of Learning Disabled Adults

		Criteria 1: Achievement		Criteria 2: Adjustment	
		Education	Vocation	Social/Emotional	Daily Living
Subgroup 1	S1	H	H	H	H
	S2	H	H	H	H
	S3	H	H	M	M
Subgroup 2	S4	M	M	H	H
	S5	M	M	H	H
	S6	M	L	H	H
Subgroup 3	S7	L	L	L	L
	S8	L	L	M	L
	S9	M	L	L	L

H = high
M = moderate
L = low

achievement: educational and vocational criteria, including level of educational attainment, annual income, rating of vocational class,[2] and eminence in field and vocational satisfaction; (2) adjustment: social/emotional functioning and daily living functioning, including rating of self-esteem, personality, and interpersonal style, as well as criteria regarding independent living skills such as driving, maintaining one's own living space, financial management, individual decision making, etc. The categories were taken from the clinical reporting structure of adults with learning disabilities developed by Blalock (1981).

It should be noted that subjects for this study were assigned to Criteria 1 (Achievement) on an a priori basis. The ratings assigned to Criteria 2 (Adjustment) were done on a post hoc basis by the investigators of the study. Table 1 illustrates subgroup assignments.

Subjects were contacted via telephone to solicit cooperation for the study. The rationale and purpose of the study were explained to them. All subjects agreed to participate; arrange-

---

2. According to the Duncan Socioeconomic Index; also found in Mercer's System of Multipluralistic Assessment (SOMPA).

ments to interview them were made on a follow-up telephone call. Subjects were told that all information collected as a result of the interview would be confidential and that interview data would be reported in aggregate as well as on an individual case basis. They were also told that discussion about specific cases would be reported in a way to protect the anonymity of subjects.

Reactions to requests for participation in the study were very favorable. Most of the subjects were very enthusiastic about sharing their stories with parents, peers, and professionals in the field of learning disabilities. They viewed their participation in the study as a unique opportunity to provide new insights, knowledge, and suggestions that might contribute to emerging philosophies, concepts, laws, and services particularly for the population of adolescents and adults with learning disabilities.

The interviews were held at a variety of sites, including the subjects' business offices and homes as well as the interviewers' business offices and homes. The duration of the interviews ranged from two and a half to three and a half hours. Most were three hours. All interviews were audiotaped with prior permission. Subjects had the option of stopping the tape at any time, but none invoked this prerogative. All interviews were transcribed from audiotapes after all of the interviews were completed. Because the authors have striven to transcribe the subjects' responses as faithfully as possible, some grammatical errors may appear in material quoted from the interviews and in the transcriptions in Appendix B.

Instrumentation

The interview format for the study followed the basic tenets of ethnographic interviewing (Spradley 1979). As in any ethnographic study, the goal was to "to grasp the native's (respondent's) point of view, his relation to life, to realize *his* vision of *his* world" (Hanson 1958). The process involves the discovery of the insider's point of view. For the purposes and theme of the study, this process focused on adults with learning disabilities speaking for themselves.

Appendix A shows the instrument used by the interviewers. As has been previously mentioned, the categories from Blalock

(1981) were used in order to gather a holistic view of the learning disabled adult experience. The data gathered through the ethnographic interview comprised the following: demographic and background information, educational history, social and emotional functioning, vocational history, daily living skills, and critical incidents from any of the areas of inquiry. Familial issues were not directly elicited, but material about the interviewee's family both while growing up and in adult life was intermixed in responses throughout the entire interview.

Description of Subject Groups and Subjects

As was indicated earlier (for the purpose of analysis), the adults with learning disabilities who participated in the study were divided into three subgroups on the basis of their commonalities (achievement criteria). A general description of the subgroups and a brief but specific profile of the subjects are provided. The subjects' past histories will be summarized in the education section of the monograph. A definition of learning disabilities elicited from each subject as part of the interview process is given in this chapter. The rationale for this action was dictated by the spirit and intent of the monograph as well as the projective uses and aspects that may be used in understanding the data individually and in toto.

Subgroup 1: Highly Adjusted to Adulthood

Subgroup 1 of adults with learning disabilities is characterized by high vocational achievement with high-status, well-paying jobs. Not only do these individuals have undergraduate degrees, but they all have graduate degrees, which are a prerequisite for the jobs they are currently performing. Two have graduate degrees from professional schools (law and dentistry). This subgroup also evidences moderate to high levels of adjustment in social/emotional and daily living functioning. Their level of socioadaptive functioning enables them to acquire the flexibility to support their vocational success as well as manage their personal and daily living schedule in a satisfactory manner.

Subject 1

Subject 1 (S1) is a fifty-six-year-old attorney, who has specialized in real estate and business law since the late 1950s. For the past decade, he has not actively practiced law but has overseen his interests and investments in commercial and residential real estate. He is a member of local, state, and national bar associations and is a fellow of the American Academy of Real Estate Attorneys. S1 is married and has seven children, some of whom are still in high school. His avocational pursuits involve board duties for a local nonprofit vocational center for citizens who are mentally retarded. In addition, he likes to sail, fish, and hunt.

Definition of learning disabilities: "Learning disabilities means determination in order to graduate from high school and college. It means accomplishment in spite of reading problems. It means encountering things which are very hard and hard keeping up."

Subject 2

Subject 2 (S2) is a thirty-nine-year-old dentist who splits his time between a private practice and a part-time appointment in the state university's dental school. He has been a dentist for the last twelve years and has been involved in dental education for the last ten years. Professional associations include local, state and national dental groups as well as higher education organizations involved with dental education. S2 is married and has three school-age children ranging from elementary to junior high school level. His leisure time is filled with family pursuits; he loves camping and vegetable gardening.

Definition of learning disabilities: "Learning disabilities can be summed up this way. There was always a certain picture on the wall that I didn't understand. One day I looked at it, and I understood everything about it. It made me feel for the first time that the world wasn't divided up with smart people and people on the other side. It means that (if you make it) you are not only street smart, but that you can be bright too."

Subject 3

Subject 3 (S3) is a twenty-eight-year-old assistant dean of students at a large urban university in the Gulf South. At the time of the interview, she was virtually an acting dean because of her supervisor's retirement. She worked in the student personnel field even before she received her master's degree in guidance and counseling. Prior to her present employment, she was successfully employed at two other universities. S3 has numerous professional memberships specifically related to her current position. She has never been married and reports to have a fairly active social life. Interests and hobbies include reading for pleasure, needle crafts, and swimming for exercise.

Definition of learning disabilities: "Because I studied it, I have changed my outlook. When I don't talk about it and let my emotions take over, it's just frustration. And that's all I can remember of my childhood and schooling. Because I've known about it so long, it is just part of my life—not a new handicap. I never viewed it as a handicap because it was always there. (On one hand) it isn't anything other than pain, frustration, and more pain. But the flipside is pats on the back because I have made it somehow."

Subgroup 2: Moderately Adjusted to Adulthood

Subgroup 2 of adults with learning disabilities can best be described as heterogeneous. Subjects are satisfactorily adjusted to both vocational and personal aspects of their lives. Their adjustment experiences have been varied. The major commonalities of this group are graduation from high school programs specifically designed for students with learning disabilities and fruitful, productive personal relationships in their adult lives. The diversity of their life experiences may be characteristic of both disabled and nondisabled groups in the after-school years. Nevertheless, these experiences are influenced by the presence of learning disabilities.

Also noteworthy of Subgroup 2 is a trend of stable relationships. Described are three varieties of personal relationships that represent marked changes in lifestyle and entry into mature, long-term commitments. Age is probably a prime factor as Subgroup 2 subjects are all in their early to late twenties.

Subject 4

Subject 4 (S4) is a twenty-four-year-old electrician. He graduated from a high school for students with learning disabilities and completed a vocational preparation program at a local community college. His adolescent life was punctuated by success in entry level jobs that he kept for prolonged periods of time. He is engaged to be married to a woman who is in her first year of medical school. Currently, S4 lives at home with his parents.

Definition of learning disabilities: "A learning disability puts boundaries on you, and that makes you realize what your limitations are. It kind of rules out all these other things you may be able to do. It kind of narrows the pathways."

Subject 5

Subject 5 (S5) is a twenty-nine-year-old mother of two preschool children. She has been married for six years. Her husband works for a major newspaper in New Orleans, where she worked before becoming a homebound mother. She and her husband own their own home. S5 graduated from a high school for students who are learning disabled and received a certificate from the county vocational-technical program in filing. At the time of the interview, she was planning to study typing and accounting at the same school. She is a bowling enthusiast and belongs to a bowling league. She describes her spare time first love as shopping.

Definition of learning disabilities: "Learning disabilities means trouble in reading and writing and frustration. People thought you were dumb or stupid or didn't want to study. It wasn't true. It is what's the matter with you. It is your limitations."

Subject 6

Subject 6 (S6) is a twenty-nine-year-old male who not only has learning disabilities but has spina bifida and is physically disabled. He is ambulatory with the help of Canadian crutches. At the time of the interview, S6 had just moved in with his girlfriend and her three children. He is employed by a fast food franchise company. His work involves delivering food to houses in the geographical area of the store.

A Louisiana native, S6 graduated from a private high school in Massachusetts and attended one year of college out of state before returning to the New Orleans area. He is an active member of the local LDA (Learning Disabilities Association) chapter and has served on its board of directors. His hobbies involve electronics as well as volunteer work for health-related organizations.

Definition of learning disabilities: "People with learning disabilities weren't born with a stamp on their forehead that says you are an LD. Everybody has a learning disability in one way or another. Everybody tries to put LD in a box. That can't be done. You have to poke some holes in the box and let some of it spread around."

Subgroup 3: Low (Marginal) Adjustment to Adulthood

The third cluster of adults with learning disabilities, Subgroup 3, comprises individuals who are marginal in their adjustment to adulthood. It is noteworthy and coincidental to the study that none have completed high school programs. This lack of formal education has been a major factor in erratic employment patterns and less than satisfactory vocational adjustment. The group ranges in age from twenty-two to thirty-three. Each of these adults lives in a sate of dependency with either a parent or spouse. This dependency has translated into reliance on their "significant other" or parent(s) for finances, and their source of social contact and stimulation is family rather than friends. (This may not be as true for S9 as for S7 and S8.) In each case, an issue emerges regarding the soundness of support systems.

Subject 7

Subject 7 (S7) is a thirty-three-year-old male who lives with his seventy year-old widowed mother. He attended numerous schools during his school-age years, from local public schools to private in-state and out-of-state schools. Initial diagnosis was suspected mental retardation, but the diagnosis evolved to a learning disabilities disorder after intensive evaluation and clinical teaching. S7 did not graduate from a high school program but only received a certificate of attendance. Although his vocational history includes success as a local truck driver (pickups and deliveries), he has more recently experienced long periods of unemployment. Avocational interests include gardening, woodworking, and studying the Bible.

Definition of learning disabilities: "You reverse words and numbers and remember. So you take a mirror and through the mirror write your name, or write something or trace something, looking through the mirror at what you're doing, ... and when you write something, it's backward, it's opposite of what you're seeing. It's reversing things, if you can imagine writing things backward. When you see things through a television camera you see things upside down and backwards, but when you see it, it is right side up."

Subject 8

Subject 8 (S8) is a twenty-six-year-old female who at the time of the study had been married for fourteen months. She is married to an electrician who works for a convention facility in a large metropolitan area. She and her husband have no children. S8 worked in entry level jobs after leaving high school without her diploma, but has not worked since her marriage. Her avocational interests include jogging and camping as well as restoring the house in which she and her husband currently live.

Definition of learning disabilities: "Not being able to catch up with other students. Not able to learn as fast. Hearing and seeing is different. Not being able to absorb the work in a workbook. Not being able to understand it."

Subject 9

Subject 9 (S9) is twenty-two years old and lives next to his mother in a town house he helped to build with his father. He is a high school dropout and has no history of sustained work experiences besides helping in his father's construction business. His current source of income is his family. Interests include stereos, cars, and tinkering with mechanical things.

Definition of learning disabilities: "Learning disabilities is really a pain in the neck. If somebody tells you something and they expect you to remember it and you can't remember it, that puts you in a serious jam."

CHAPTER 3
Educational

Subgroup 1

S1

In the case of S1, the major difficulty throughout his education was a severe reading problem that can be described clinically as dyslexia. This problem evidenced itself in the earliest years of grade school and persisted through his law training many years later. Painful recollections of negative reading experiences date as far back as third grade. S1 related the intensity of shame and embarrassment during this time. "I remember times in third grade when Sister M. A. would scream and holler at me when I was standing up in the classroom because I couldn't read the reader. And I was standing there and the print was in front of me, but I just couldn't read it. And I can remember feeling completely helpless and feeling lost—feeling put upon and feeling bad in the eyes of the other children because they thought I was a failure."

The struggle of learning to read was not mitigated with time or remediation, however. Grade school and middle school years were the most frustrating. Each grade proved to be as difficult as the previous grade, and assignments did not get any easier. Over time there grew a repertoire of compensatory strategies that proved not only useful but indispensable. These strategies became the wherewithal to land S1 not only in a parochial high school that catered to academically elite students but also in an honors track. Despite the significant reading problems, S1 knew he could succeed because he would not have found himself in such a selective program otherwise. Moreover, this knowledge gave him the confidence to push on and compete. "I knew I had a reasonably high IQ and that I was able to cope and compensate for some of my deficiencies in not being able to read. It meant having to read the same poem four times instead of once. It meant having to study six hours in an evening instead of two hours like everybody else did."

The educational experience of S1 was fraught with anxiety. This anxiety permeated school assignments and homework. Encouragement and tutoring within the household from parents and a revered aunt offset some of this anxiety. Encouragement was also given in school, particularly by math teachers who recognized talent in that academic area. Ironically, there was little chastisement from peers throughout S1's school years, but teachers often teased him, and parents set S1 apart from other siblings in the family because of his inability to read. He received mixed messages from his support systems, but a burning desire to excel always remained with him. This burning desire was quite evident later in his law education.

The experience in law school was no different than any other S1 had encountered in earlier years. The choice of law was made over physics because "chemistry did me in." Law seemed to have more practicality, especially as it related to business. Many extra hours were spent reading law books. Many evenings were spent locked up in the law library. Study strategies were cleverly devised. S1 learned how to skim cases, so that the central issue could be discerned by reading two paragraphs instead of sixteen pages. Outlining and key notes were substituted for rereading each case. It is here that S1 believes his analytical skills were sharpened. When necessary, cases were read over and over until they were understood. S1 was used to working longer and harder, which he described as a chore. "When I was in law school, there were not a whole lot of options. By that time I was so used to it, if there were four books to read, it was not a question of whether I was going to read the four books, it was the question of how I was going to read the four books."

The educational experience of S1 was marked by outstanding accomplishment achieved through extreme determination. He admitted that the price was one that sacrificed social development and the typical adventures and experiences of childhood. Some of these aspects labeled as "scar tissue" by S1 are developed in the section dealing with social and emotional functioning.

S2

The educational experiences of S2 can best be described as atypical from grade school through his years of dental education. Throughout his schooling, there was an omnipresent feeling of being unique among his peers, as well as the recognition that he accomplished developmental and educational tasks in a different manner. In sum, the accumulation of experiences created a problem of poor academic self-concept that persisted even to his final days of dental school. A recollection of his grade school experience reveals that S2 was able "to get a grasp on [his] learning disability" sometime around third grade. Prior to that time, S2 recalls that he was unable to track school tasks and activities. In his words, he was "too young to understand what was going on except I was not able to do what others could." Furthermore, he was often accused of daydreaming, not paying attention, and being careless. At the same time, S2 knew that "something was wrong." "Other people could appreciate all sorts of things I could not. It depressed me that other kids could read and understand things on a page, and that I had no idea of what was going on."

Moreover, at the time he was attending grade school he was never formally labeled learning disabled—but "everybody knew [he] had problems." His parents thought that "something was out of kilter." S2 received much tutoring from his family and from private tutors while always staying in a regular education class. Yet, he progressed academically, and that took the focus off of him and put it on his younger brother, who, at the first sign of a problem, almost immediately underwent psychological testing for significant learning problems. S2 recollected that his parents took his problem quite seriously after "they realized he wasn't a genius." S2 knew intuitively that if he was going to make it, it would have to be done by hard work. An example of that spirit is his recollection that "I tried and I just tried to be more careful whatever I did, and eventually I got it to where it was acceptable."

This realization was internalized early on in his education and proved to be a source of strength since third grade. It became apparent that if he wanted something, he would have to work extra hard to achieve it. But he could only achieve if he were given the time. "If I have enough time I know I can do it." That thought alone has given S2 confidence to achieve the things he wanted to accomplish at all levels of his education.

When S2 entered junior high school, he saw students who had more severe learning problems than he had. This helped him accomplish his work, for he gained much inner strength from realizing that he did not have it "that bad." Two teachers had a dramatic impact on him while in eighth grade. His math teacher gave him many problems focusing on repetition of basic operations. Not only did this help a great deal, but he became very adept at following columns and keeping place value. His reading teacher gave him numerous workbook assignments that required him to write out answers to questions, all in a timed format. In retrospect, S2 views these teachers as "not necessarily being good teachers, but they always were able to hit upon things that worked."

S2 does not report any significant recollections about grades nine through twelve. He had problems in French class but encountered no other hurdles. In fact, S2 described these years as being devoid of challenge and even commented that "high school was a joke." At that time, however, S2 was doing much on his own to master his high school experience. He said, "I had to persevere and self-organize because I knew I had to persevere or I would not make it. My ambition was to keep going even though I did not like school very much. Actually, to this day I am still not crazy about it."

There is an interesting paradox to S2's transition from high school to college. Despite finishing high school and entering the flagship university of his state, he had a puzzling comment. "It was tough to constantly fail at something I was expected to be good at. When you get into that cycle, it's hard to pull yourself out." Yet, he found himself experiencing success early on. In his first biology course, he took a difficult examination and received a B − . At this a fellow student commented that he must be very smart to get a B. The next class after the examination most of the lecture auditorium was empty. It was then that he said to himself, "Smart, yeah, I must be." Undergraduate courses were quite challenging. Science was difficult, but foreign languages (as in high school) were nearly impossible. Early on in his undergraduate studies, he learned that higher education would not be easy. This was true of his dental education. In sum, S2 said, "I just really worked hard to get through."

S2 reported that dental school defined clearly what the strengths and weaknesses of his disability were. He was good in abstract reasoning and spatial relationships but very poor in visual discrimination. He had more than adequate ability in fine motor tasks, as evidenced by his success on the chalk carving part of the Dental Aptitude Test. (Chalk carving is no longer a part of the Dental Aptitude Test.) All in all, he did well on the Dental Aptitude Test. This led him to exclude from vocational consideration engineering, medicine, and veterinary medicine. However, his love for biology propelled him into a health career, and denistry held the most interest and promise.

S2 attended a dental school in the Washington, D.C., area. He reported that after two years everything fell into place. "I would do what I would have to do. I would get home and study as long as I could. Then I would *hope* for the best. I would study in intervals (ten to fifteen minutes) of concentrated study. I had trouble concentrating for more than fifteen minutes. But luckily I had a terrific memory. Once it gets in there, it does not get out."

It was not easy, but it was "do-able." The dental curriculum mixed dental students with medical students and postgraduate science and allied health students. Tests were tough, but S2 always managed to stay "at least in the middle" when it came to grades. This he attributes to multiple choice questions that required little writing and deemphasized needed spelling skills.

After completing his dental education, S2 returned to the greater New Orleans area to become a practicing dentist. Of note is that S2 had two brothers who were diagnosed as learning disabled. When asked why he succeeded and his brothers did not, he simply replied, "Perhaps I was able to succeed a little bit earlier academically than they did."

S3

The educational experiences of S3 are sketchy in her mind prior to the seventh grade. Most recollections associated with the

learning process during her grade school years are blurred. S3
describes herself as a rebel in her early school years. She even
got kicked out of school because of her opposition to school
policies. These stands did yield gains, however, because she bol-
stered her popularity and fortified her leadership standing with
her peers—peers that were described in the interview as being
relatively smart.

There was always the feeling of being dumb. S3 felt "dumb
all the time." The only positive experience recalled was in fourth
grade. It was there that S3 remembers a supportive teacher. This
was the only teacher who understood her problem. During her
time in fourth grade, "the basics were stressed and appreciated."
S3 recounted:

> She used to let me do little afternoon school projects that
> most kids would consider demerits. I would clean erasers and
> do things like that. I couldn't get my letters to go in order.
> I knew the tune but I certainly didn't know how the letters
> went. And I remember in fourth grade playing and clapping
> erasers, singing the alphabet and rhyming—cat, bat, hat,
> sat—those kinds of things with her. And she made a lot of
> sense, all after school. That is the only time in school I can
> look back and say that's a good memory.

It was during her year in seventh grade that learning disabilities were confirmed. There was no special class placement
for S3 because the only available special educational class in her
school was one for mentally retarded children. The explanation
of the learning problem was "you cannot read," and she responded, "I have been telling everybody I cannot read for years."
At the time of the testing, S3 was attending summer school.
She entered seventh grade reading at a third grade level, with
the total inability to spell even the easiest word. At that point,
it was evident that "I was not dumb." Her deviant behavior
stemmed from her frustration and need for attention.

The diagnosis of learning disabilities did not change the attitude of S3's parents. As she recalls, "Neither of my parents
accepted my problem. Neither was involved in my education.
They didn't go to PTA meetings and they didn't go to school

functions because it was embarrassing and negative for my family, especially my father." Doctors said that S3 would grow out of her problem, but that did not happen. Consequently, S3's parents sought out tutoring.

Tutoring began during her seventh grade year. Why tutoring was not sought earlier is a mystery to S3. After she started with the tutor, several neighbors started sending their children to the same tutor. This helped to mitigate any stigma. S3 recounted, "I was never alone. We all went to the same tutor at different times, and after one would go, the other, etc. So it was not as if I were doing something on my own. We had a lot of dumb kids on my block." Her first tutor was not very helpful. The tutor wanted to counsel, and S3 wanted to learn to read. So the tutor was replaced by an older woman and "that made all the difference in the world."

S3's tutor served as more than just an academic tutor, however. As rapport developed, S3 found that she valued the emotional support her tutor provided. Tutoring sessions became mini-counseling sessions, and these proved very beneficial. This experience diminished much tension and helped motivate S3 to work harder in school and study more at home. This apparently was not enough, however. The tutor notified S3's family that she would need extra help from her parents in order to progress. This suggestion caused resentment toward the tutor, who was getting paid to be the tutor. The family reaction was, "She's not retarded, so why can't she do it?"

The tutor helped S3 throughout high school. But a complicating factor had developed. S3 had acquired a severe drinking problem. She readily admitted, "I don't remember working harder in high school because most of the time I was drunk. And I spent a lot of time covering up so that no one knew I had a problem." One of S3's major recollections about high school was doing work for her tutor. (She does not remember doing school work.) The efforts of the tutor proved very helpful, too, even beyond S3's school years. "I really got a big jump on how to study appropriately. I used this all the way through my master's degree. There's still things that I read that I still don't know what they mean, but I know how to study for them and I can do it." S3 reported that she has always had a good sight memory that helps her a great deal. This too was developed through working with her tutor.

Upon graduation from high school, a debate emerged about S3's future. Her mother thought that she would become a secretary, but S3 was adamant about going to college. All her friends were going to college, and her sister had gone to college before her. When her mother insisted that S3 was not going to do well, she responded, "So I'll flunk out and I'll come home. But I'll pay. I want to go. I do not want to stay home." S3's past successes coupled with her determination ultimately convinced her family to let her go. She had already developed a track record by working (and making good money) as the manager of a specialty department in a department store; she had been doing the grocery shopping for her household; and she participated equally, and often played a dominant role, when it came to family decisions.

The choice of a college that fit her situation was of paramount importance. S3 was "determined to succeed." She reasoned that she could not get into the two major state universities but could start at a university with lower standards. She explained, "I knew that if I was in a place that I failed I could get home quick enough, and knew if my parents needed me they could get to me quick enough. And I knew I was bound to have academic success because it was the easiest university in the state."

S3 chose special education as a major and with luck was assigned a major professor whose specialty was learning disabilities. This association helped greatly. At times her professor was more lenient, but that was because "she knew what I was going through." The most difficult time in undergraduate school was the freshman year. The drinking problem from high school had carried over. S3 does not have any recollections of that year, much less of how she passed. S3 admitted it was overcompensation in the form of drinking that almost did her in. S3 received mostly B's during her undergraduate years. She did well in education courses and courses in which she knew she would be successful. This success mitigated her drinking problem, and eventually drinking totally vanished from her daily life. However, she always had an extremely difficult time with written assignments.

Upon completion of her undergraduate degree, she entered a master's program in counseling and finished in one and a half years instead of two. Grades became secondary, while still being the most depressing part of school. Learning was most important. This contrasted to earlier times when report cards sent home and parents' signatures were horrendous experiences. She had also become a graduate assistant, which aided in providing practical experience to her counseling program. It was a very fulfilling educational experience. S3 recounted, "I did real well. Academically, it wasn't very difficult because I really liked what I was studying.... I knew I spent a lot of time studying, but I was never caught behind. Only I had to get extensions on my papers."

Writing papers was always the most traumatic part of graduate school for S3. Typing was a skill that she was not able to master. "It took me so long when I was young to learn the alphabet in order, that to learn a keyboard out of order was very confusing for me." However, she compensated by having a cooperative roommate proofread and type her papers. Writing in-class essays would have been even more problematic, but she did have one professor who let her circle her words she thought she couldn't spell so that she could look them up in the *Bad Speller's Dictionary.*

At the time this study was in progress, S3 was planning to enter a doctoral program in counseling at the university at which she was working. Major hurdles that were anticipated were the Graduate Record Examination entrance requirement, writing term papers, and writing a dissertation. But these are the same hurdles she has seen before. She expects to deal with those hurdles similar to the way in which she dealt with the hurdles she experienced in her previous years.

Education Summary for Subgroup 1

One of the a priori criteria for assignment to Subgroup 1 was a high level of education, a characteristic shared by S1, S2, and

S3. All had difficult times with academic demands during their schooling, but none experienced difficulty to the degree of requiring specialized classes or programs. Even though they stayed in regular education classes throughout their schooling, they all needed some tutorial help to be successful.

The theme of success begetting success is particularly germane to the educational experiences of the members of Subgroup 1. Each had successes along the way to remind themselves that they were not stupid or incompetent. They used past successful experiences to get through the tough times. Interwoven with their success pattern was a willingness to work extra hard to achieve more success. They were willing to spend longer, sometimes much longer, time to accomplish what others could do relatively easily. Any attempt to pinpoint the source of this motivation necessitates recognizing the interaction of a wide array of variables. A combination of innate desire with an environment that somehow communicated the importance of achievement undoubtedly spurred a hard-work ethic. Additionally, part of the drive to succeed arose from the desire to avoid shame and embarrassment in school. All members of Subgroup 1 had strong family support for their education. S3 apparently had the most equivocal family support, and each reported feeling pressure from their family's expectations for academic success.

Success in school carried an explicit price tag for S1 and an implicit one for all the subjects in Subgroup 1. S1 stated several times that his social skills and social life suffered irreparable damage because of his self-imposed isolation for studying. S2 was virtually a prisoner to his studies at dental school, and S3 saw her determination as bordering on obsessive. Nevertheless, the successful educational experiences of Subgroup 1 translated overall into a foundation for successful adult adaptation, especially successful vocational achievement.

Subgroup 2

S4

S4 began his school career in a large urban school system. All in all, he attended eighteen public schools, even attending seven schools in one year. It was quite obvious that his case was a unique one. Diagnostic personnel kept insisting on a diagnosis of mental retardation, but his performance belied this label as a true description of his intellectual capacity. S4 remembers, "I knew I was not like that. Also, the teacher saw how I performed, and she knew I was not mentally retarded. But I was in that class for two weeks." All along his parents were very supportive of him. They urged him not to panic while they battled school authorities and teachers behind the scenes. In fact, S4 did not panic and recounted a critical incident that had a great impact at that time.

In third grade, his father took him to a rifle range for a weekend outing. At that time, he had never fired a rifle before. He did very well that day—as well as others who had had more experience. He came to the realization that he was not mentally retarded and that he was capable of higher skills and abilities. S4 stated that he derives a lot of strength from this experience.

He entered fifth grade in a private school for students with learning disabilities and other learning problems. One of his first thoughts upon entering the school was that all the students looked normal and were even physically attractive. From there on out his educational life became more positive. S4 described the manifestations of his learning disabilities upon entering the private school for students with learning disabilities. "I could read, not well, but proficiently. I could not spell a word even though I could read it off a piece of paper. When it came to writing it, I could not spell it. I had very high auditory comprehension. And that was my biggest problem getting placed in school. Orally, I can almost mimic what I've just read, but when it comes to writing it down I cannot get close to the ball park. Reading and telling (about the story) I get almost perfect; writing I can't."

It was in this special educational placement that S4 began to progress dramatically. The educational philosophy and instructional approach fit S4 well. "They had the ability to meet everyone on his/her own level. I was good in math but had a terrible time with reading. That is where they taught me on my level. They could define your problem and not hold you back in all areas (i.e., arithmetic) but focus on that problem at your own pace."

In the estimation of S4, his education after placement in private school was very valuable. They treated him "as if I were normal" with a learning disability. He could not offer the same comment about the public schools. Upon graduation from the high school program, S4 was counseled not to go to a four-year college but to attend a junior college first. Those who gave him advice told him he had more potential than aspiring to a career such as managing a Burger King. This was the extent of transitional counseling at that time. From his date of graduation until the following December, he worked at the same restaurant that he worked in during his high school years. Then S4 began looking into the local vocational-technical school programs, but viewed them as having inadequate teachers and facilities. Ultimately, he attended the junior college but had not the slightest idea of what to study. A period of investigating careers followed, which led to a decision to go into a trade-oriented field. After ruling out the things he could not do, he started at the beginning of the junior college catalogue and went from there. As S4 put it, "I went from A to Z and stopped at E." It was then that he decided to go into electronics. He tried electronics, especially as it applied to computers, but balked because of his inability to learn the material by reading. Then he settled on training to be an electrician. In his earlier years he had bigger dreams, but S4 will be the first to say these dreams were not compatible with his abilities.

In his first class in junior college, he told the instructor that he had learning disabilities. S4 recounted, "That was the biggest mistake of my life." The instructor started treating S4 as if he were mentally retarded, which evoked bad memories from his public school experience. Ironically, his teacher then helped S4 to pass his courses. He simplified tests for S4, and he went as far as to write down words needed to answer questions on tests without giving him the answers themselves. In that way S4 was able to spell the words correctly when answering examination questions. For his certification test to be an electrician he was allowed to use his textbooks. The focus of the examination was application and utilization of the electrician's code book. Therefore, the requirements for certification capitalized on his abilities while not needlessly exposing his weaknesses. It took S4 two years, attending classes four days a week, to complete his courses. He started the course of study with forty plus students. At the end of the first semester, there were fifteen students, and at the end of the program, only about five students were certifiable. He reflected on his career choice and training. "I knew I could be somebody. . . . And I knew way back that college may be out of reach for me. So I needed to get a trade or something, a good trade, a solid trade. And that's what I have been working and trying to do since the day I got out of high school. I finally found something that fit."

S5

S5 began her education in a Catholic school located in the metropolitan area. As early as first grade, S5 was having problems in preacademic tasks and reading readiness activities. These problems became evident to S5's parents as she had more and more difficulty with her homework. It was during third grade that S5's parents received a telephone call from the principal telling them that S5 was mentally retarded and that the school had made arrangements to send her to a school for mentally retarded children. With this action S5's parents became upset and sought psychological testing and consultation for their daughter. The psychologist who evaluated S5 concluded that she, in fact, had learning disabilities and that she should not be placed with mentally retarded children. Soon after, S5 was placed in a public school setting to receive special education services. Although this was not the most ideal placement for S5, the programming fit her learning problems.

S5 remembers quite vividly how she was never able to fit in. "The problem was that in first grade they were trying to teach me English and Spanish, and I could not get English, much less Spanish. The school was too advanced, and I did not fit in. I was very frustrated. I'll never forget spelling bees and being the first one out. That was very frustrating. I would have a simple word and mess it up by reversing the letters." S5's main problems throughout her grade school years were all aspects of reading and spelling.

S5 recounted that throughout her years in public school placement she suffered from low self-confidence. She remembers failing tests even when students were asked to pick from answers listed on the blackboard. However, she began to realize in junior high school that she was good in math. She could handle "more complicated stuff." No longer did she think she was stupid, and she was convinced that she was not retarded. What was confusing to her was how she could do well in a subject like math and be bad in five others. She often asked herself, "If I can do math, why can't I do this?"

S5 made a dramatic turn when she entered a private school for students with learning disabilities at the beginning of her sophomore year of high school. It seems that every aspect of her new school fit perfectly with her psychoeducational needs. She recalled that her confidence developed rapidly. Everything about the school was good in her opinion. There were smaller classes and substantially more individual attention. "They had much more time to spend with you when you were doing something wrong, like reading." S5 went on to say, "We all had the same thing wrong, and the teachers were sympathetic. They knew we had a problem, and they took their time explaining it. . . . They would read it, then discuss it, and then give the assignment."

Her new school program soon began to yield good grades and an accompanying feeling of confidence regarding her academic subjects. She admitted that her new placement made her feel smart. She was accustomed to bringing home report cards with C's and D's and a couple of F's. She recounted her reaction to bringing home a good report card. The report card had A's and B's, and her first comment to her mother was, "Momma, look A's! I now know what they look like." Her parents were not only surprised, but excited. S5 did so well in her new educational placement that she graduated at the end of her junior year. She was able to matriculate early by attending summer school and accumulating some credits through a study tour in Europe. In retrospect, S5 said she should have stayed another year in school. It would have allowed for more time to acquire additional skills and perhaps given her more valuable time to plan her transition to the world of work via meaningful post-secondary study.

Upon graduation, S5 went to a local community college. She went simply because she had received a letter from the community college's recruiting office before graduating from high school. In fact, she was the only one who received the letter of invitation, which was quite flattering to her. She entered the community college but pursued a different program of study than the one she was originally invited to attend, which she concluded was really not for her. "It was more for kids that had handicaps—like paralyzed, blind, and physically impaired, not kids who were slow."

The program she entered taught her school and office work. She did not attempt to learn word processing; however, she decided that she wanted to pursue a career in computers. She recalled, "At the time, I wanted to get into computers. And they said, 'You will not be able to do that. It's too complicated. If you don't have the support of your counselor, then forget it.' I should not have listened to them."

The only job that her program prepared her for was that of cashier. She believes she could have learned this job on her own. She did not become a cashier either. Soon after leaving her community college program, she got a job at a metropolitan newspaper (through answering an advertisement in the classified ads) and subsequently enrolled in a filing course at a vocational-technical school in order to help her with her work. She completed her course satisfactorily but not without a bad experience reminiscent of her earlier days in school. She remembered being most anxious in this educational setting because she had an "older teacher who believed in teaching by having the students read out loud." This was a failure experience that she would like to forget but is still unable to do so.

S5 plans to educate herself further. This must be done while raising her children, however. Learning disabilities do not hold her back nor does she look upon her past educational accomplishments as a victory. The fact that she is trying to go back to school is to a large degree a vindication of her spirit. She is at a point in her life where she wants to pick her own course of study because she herself knows best what her interests are and how they match her abilities.

S6

A confounding factor of S6's educational experience is that he not only has learning disabilities, but he is also physically disabled (spina bifida). Spina bifida only contributed indirectly to his educational problems, while learning disabilities were always paramount when designing and providing educational and special educational services. However, spina bifida was a constant source of poor prognosis, which became a rallying point for both S6 and his parents.

S6's educational history from the time he entered grammar school in Louisiana until he graduated from high school in Boston was complicated. He first attended a Catholic grammar school whose principal told S6's parents that he was having significant problems with comprehension (auditory and reading). At that point, he was evaluated at both a university clinic and a major university medical center. The tests, which took several months to complete, yielded a diagnosis of learning disabilities with severe comprehension problems and reversal problems in reading. S6 then was placed for a half day in his regular classroom and for a half day in a special class in the same school. This arrangement did not prove to be satisfactory.

S6 remembered quite well a critical incident during his early grade school years: "I got tired of being told when I was in grammar school that I was not going to amount to anybody. And my problem was that I never understood what I would read in school. This even prompted one of my teachers to tell my mother I was mentally retarded. My mom came home and told me. But she said I had too beautiful a mind and too much understanding to be mentally retarded."

In fact, some of his teachers were convinced he was mentally retarded and were very complacent about his slow progress. S6 remembered seeing many of his classmates "passing me up" while he was held back in his present grade. His recollection of his combined regular and special education experiences provides a poignant description of his learning disabilities.

For homework I would read a book and write a composition of what I read. I would get my pencil and paper and write what I thought was coming out of the book. And my stories were totally different than the stories I had read. And my teachers would say, "Well see, you write some good stories, but you were supposed to read what was in this book." And I said, "Hey, I read what was in the book, and this is what I comprehended." That's when they started questioning, "Why does he get a totally different story?" And what I was doing was I was able to read the words—I was able to read those in the book. But in the time it went from the book to my brain, it got lost somewhere.

Math was not a problem for S6. He reported that he never reversed numbers or number operations. Word problems were particularly difficult, however.

Since his educational situation was less than satisfactory, S6 was reevaluated about one year after his first evaluation. He was then placed in a number of private schools for students with learning disabilities and learning problems. These placements tended to meet his psychoeducational needs.

S6's mother kept searching for an even better educational environment. Through an informal network of parents with children who were learning disabled, she had heard very favorable reviews of a summer program at a military academy in Georgia. She traveled to Georgia and met with the executive director of the academy, a man with a Ph.D. in educational psychology, who was owner of the school. At first the director was reticent about the idea of S6 attending the school because of his physical disability. It was agreed, "If he made it, then he made it; if not, at least he was able to make a go of it." (S6 recounted in retrospect that most schools he attended were not accustomed to physically disabled students with learning problems who were nevertheless able to learn with able-bodied students.)

S6 attended the military school for two summer sessions in two consecutive years. At first the idea of living away from home was overwhelming for S6, but in retrospect he agrees it was a very positive part of his educational experience. The program was highly structured in both academic and nonacademic activities. His teachers took him back to the first letter of the alphabet and the first number of the number system. "They even used a 'scratch board' that if you miss something, you do it with your finger." In S6's words, "It was horrible. It was tragic." Then all of a sudden he had what seemed to be a magical experience.

"One day I discovered that I could actually read and understand what was going on. I went home and told my mom, 'Hey, I can do it, I can read.' That's when the ball started rolling." This set the stage for attendance at a private school for students with learning disabilities outside of Boston, Massachusetts. He graduated from that school after a couple of years of attendance at age twenty.

S6 never attended a college program after his completion of high school, but has undertaken other postsecondary training. None of his training has actually led to entrance into a profession or trade. He attended a community college program and earned nearly a year's worth of college credit. He has also taken electronics courses. At the time of the interview, S6 was trying to enter a program to train to be an X-ray technician. Initially, he was dissuaded from entering the program because of his physical disability. There was great concern over his ability to push equipment and aid in the positioning of patients. S6 is determined to reapply to the program. He immodestly commented that employment in a hospital setting is his forte because he has spent so much time in a hospital during his life. Yet, the kind of job he wants necessitates further education.

Education Summary for Subgroup 2

The members of this subgroup all experienced a number of educational placements, exemplified most dramatically by S4's placement in eighteen different schools or classes. All had significant difficulty in elementary school. Often, they were not in special programs, and when they were, the methods of instruction and remediation were ineffective. In contrast, they all related positive experiences to their education in special programs. These programs may have provided an environment for important educational successes and social skill development. Both S4 and

S6 have had success with postsecondary training, and S5 is contemplating furthering her education.

Successful school experiences elicited overwhelmingly positive reactions in Subgroup 2 and may explain how they managed to succeed in competitive employment in spite of an absence of transitional services. All felt that the reading and language skills acquired in the specialized programs opened up the adult world by allowing them to participate in activities requiring reading. The eventual placement in effective (and expensive) programs evidences family support for all members of Subgroup 2. In each case, the family never gave up on their child with learning disabilities.

Subgroup 3 Education

S7

The education of S7 was marked by a state of disequilibrium in educational placement and program. It seems as if there was a different school each year and each school was further and further from home. S7 began his education in a neighborhood preschool class. He then attended a public school program for first grade, where his teachers discovered that he had significant developmental problems. Through the initiative of his parents (his mother was a nurse), he spent his second grade year in a private school, yet not one geared particularly for special educational programs. In third and fourth grade, he attended a private Baptist school "which knew about his learning problems and helped as much as they could." Then began placements in private special education schools. He was first placed in a special education school that had as the majority of its population lower functioning students. S7 recalled saying to his mother after spending a short time there, "Hey mom, I don't belong here." Further psychological testing and consultation suggested that S7 be placed with children who had similar problems.

With a confirmed diagnosis of learning disabilities, S7 was placed by his parents in a private school that had, as one of its major focuses, programming for students with learning disabilities. He was so far behind in the acquisition of his basic and academic skills that there was always an urgency to make up for lost time. Of all the placements, this seemed to be the least fitting for S7's educational needs. He reflected on his feelings about that placement. "That was more than I could take . . . I felt like I was failed back to childhood . . . Like going to college and saying you have to go back to first grade." S7 stayed in this school for only one year.

The following year, S7 found himself in a private residential school in eastern Texas. By his own admission, this was his best educational experience. In that placement, he received counseling and always had ready access to doctors and psychologists whom he found to be interested in his case. He had an individual program designed for him after he underwent six months of tests. The staff was always attuned to the needs of the students. S7 recalled, "Every time you sneeze, they check you out. Did EEG's and all that stuff." S7 graduated from this program when he was seventeen. He received a diploma, but soon before he was interviewed (more than ten years later), he found out that it was a diploma signifying the completion only of eighth grade work. S7 said that he and his parents always thought he had earned a high school diploma. He is filled with remorse in retrospect that he had not gone further and had "only gone half way."

There was very little schooling after he came back home from Texas. He attended a vocational-technical school for a short time but did not acquire any additional skills. Later, he entered a woodworking course but received the lowest grade of all those enrolled in the course.

When looking back on his entire school experience, S7 commented, "What they were doing, they thought was right. I should have had it done earlier and more often or continue until today, continue training. . . . I'm not college material. . . . If they had some kind of . . . program where they could train me. . . . You could learn to support yourself." At the time of S7's interview, he was not only unemployed but had no plans to further his education.

S8

S8 began her school years in a private preschool and kindergarten. She entered first grade in a Catholic grade school and went as far as grade three in that school. This first experience with schooling was not a smooth process, however. She repeated first grade and had severe problems in mastering the developmental skills in reading, spelling, and arithmetic. At the age of eight, she ws evaluated by a clinical psychologist who discovered she was learning disabled. She was then placed in a private school that specialized in programming for children with learning disabilities. She stayed in that school until age fourteen.

S8 described her educational problems as she remembered them during that time. "If everybody had not told me that I was special and different, then maybe it would not have bothered me so much. And then not catching on fast started to bother me. I guess that I was too anxious, and then I would get frustrated. Then I would not catch on, and I would get more frustrated. Then I would get real angry, and I would walk away. Then they put me on Ritalin so I could concentrate, but still then I could not catch on so I got more frustrated."

However, S8 recalled, "I never thought of myself as dumb." There were painful moments when her friends progressed faster than she did. She also read about her problem and discovered that "a lot of bright people were learning disabled like Benjamin Franklin and Bruce Jenner." Moreover, she felt that she had more common sense than most of her classmates. As she said, "That proved that I was not dumb. I saw how the other smart kids did not have common sense. They were always doing things they got in trouble for."

S8 does not look back on her years nine through fourteen with great fondness. Of the five years that she was placed in the special school for students with learning disabilities, she mainly remembers being protected. She does recall learning some basic skills. She said, "I was separated at that school.... And I do not think it was good that I was separated from regular kids. As a result, I had trouble communicating because of the narrow life I had there."

During the time she was in her first special education placement, S8 did enjoy strong support from her parents. Her mother was a regular education teacher and was very sensitive to the needs of children who had learning problems. That is where S8 learned about famous people who had learning disabilities. S8 recalled that her mother was "always understanding and helping while trying to humor the situation when things got tough." S8 feels that her mother always treated her fairly.

S9

S9 began his education in an exclusive private day school but attended only first and second grade there. It was during second grade that S9 climbed a tree, fell out, and landed head first. He was hospitalized with a concussion at that time. In retrospect, it seemed to be the beginning of his problems. "That's probably what screwed me up." He failed second grade. Not understanding the problem, his parents sought private testing. S9 was diagnosed as having dyslexia, and he was formally labeled as having learning disabilities.

He left his original school and entered another private school that served students with learning and behavior problems. Either before or during that placement (unclear in interview), he was taken to another school for possible placement. There he encountered a different philosophy. "They said I could not listen to music, and I said what does that have to do with it? I was interested in music at that time, and I was not about to quit listening to music."

S9 attended special educational programs from second to seventh grade. He stated that he always just barely passed with C − 's and D + 's. He was unable to recollect specifically what his academic problems were. "I do not know what my problems were. I cannot remember. It's just a feeling. I think I had problems with orders and directions. I would get them twisted around, and it would be like pressure on me. As a result, I would break out of it, and I would blow it off. I just would not do anything about it."

Beginning in eighth grade, S9 was placed in another private school for students with disabilities. The classes were small, and he responded to their program. He said, "For the first time I got reading in eighth grade, and I was pretty good in English too. It was the same thing every year so I got used to it. I failed chemistry because I couldn't deal with the signs and stuff. I just failed which was okay because I did not think I needed it. Then I took remedial courses like refresh your memory in math and a little bit of reading and English." He fell further and further behind in his school work and Carnegie units. Moreover, he elected not to attend summer school to make his work up and finally dropped out of school. When asked what happened, in retrospect S9 recalled several experiences. "I would never take notes. I was not good at writing, and I would never take notes because I knew I could not keep up with the teacher. I would usually try to make it without notes. . . . I was overwhelmed by school because I felt like I could not do it. I was not quite capable . . . too much pressure. I cannot even describe it."

S9 left school and entered a vocational-technical school with the goal of getting his GED (Graduation Equivalency Diploma). S9 reported that he received his G.E.D. but had problems in his vocational training not central to his academic deficiencies. His problems were more related to his lax attitude than to his classroom performance per se. "I could not stand getting up at seven in the morning. I was usually late. Then at lunch time I would get involved in something else and not want to come back. This all stemmed from not wanting to pass and not putting what I should into it. . . . I just wanted to learn, I did not want to pass. My mechanical career went down the tubes then."

After getting "kicked out" of the local vocational-technical school, S9 entered another program to learn about auto mechanics. Along with auto mechanics courses, he was obliged to take remedial English and math courses. When asked if he attended those classes, he readily admitted, "I did not."

Education Summary for Subgroup 3

Individuals assigned to Subgroup 3 shared less than adequate educational experiences and concomitant academic deficits. None finished high school. As a result, the chances for skilled employment were limited. S8 and S9 clearly indicated that they had enjoyed little about their schooling; S7 was perhaps less adamant but expressed disappointment in his overall education and was particularly miffed that he had been led to believe that his certificate was a valid high school diploma. All members of this group have aspired to attaining some kind of high school diploma although none had organized plans to realize this goal.

The theme that emerges from the educational experiences of Subgroup 3 is one of failure begetting more failure, low academic self-confidence, and a tendency toward learned helplessness. To an extent, the members of Subgroup 3 float through the adult world, not feeling particularly in control and often being overwhelmed by the limitations of their disabilities. Their adult lives resemble their educational experiences insofar as both have been marked by frequent bouts with frustration, disappointment, and depression.

Education Summary across all Subgroups

Commonalities are scarce among the subgroups in terms of education. The one commonality that exists across all subgroups is that the educational experience was difficult for all, even for those individuals who experienced success. The degree of difficulty varied with the individual and is somewhat reflected by the attained level of education (i.e., college, high school, or unable to finish high school).

Since both innate intelligence and degree of disability are salient factors for educational prognosis, it seems reasonable to infer that these factors may be reflected in group membership. On the basis of clinical judgment (i.e., the interviewers' interaction with the subjects), the members of Subgroup 3 seem to be more disabled and certainly less verbal than any of the other subjects. Regardless of the degree of disability, Subgroup 1 members have clearly shown themselves to be very bright individuals on the basis of their educational achievements alone. Subgroup 2 members may be just as bright but more disabled, or just as disabled but less bright. Additionally, inherent individual differences such as attitude, motivation, and learning styles undoubtedly compound the reasons for educational differences across (and within) the subgroups.

CHAPTER 4

Vocational

Subgroup 1

S1

Although S1 wanted to be a physicist, law seemed to be more promising. He thought that he had an aptitude for it, and his self-assessment proved correct. Upon graduation from law school, S1 began working for a small law firm for which he had clerked during his last year of law school. After several years, he decided to start his own law firm so he could become more focused in his law practice. He developed a specialty in real estate law and soon after became instrumental in a number of transactions that made his clients large amounts of money. From these early successes in real estate law, he figured he could make money for himself, and so he set himself a goal. "Within five years, I made myself my own best client." In actuality, it took more than five years, but by that time he found that he did not have to rely on law but could concentrate more on his own real estate investments. These early successes and the general accomplishment of goals that are set for himself and his working group have provided a sense of well-being about self.

The severe reading difficulties posed problems early on in his law practice. He found trial law to be particularly stressful. He related, "I would be anxious that I'd have to read a document with people around, and I knew I couldn't do it. So I was *always* overprepared." As his law practice and businesses have become more established, he has learned to compensate for his weaknesses in reading by hiring a highly competent staff. Associates and assistants do most of his law and business reading. He explained, "To this day, now that I'm out of trial practice, I have a lady in particular who has been with me for seventeen years and who in effect is my reading eye. If I have to read under pressure, I go off to my office and deal with it."

During the developing years of his practice and business, S1 used to read everything in order to keep up. He recollected, "I was constantly anxious, and I was constantly under the gun because there were a lot of things that I had to read. . . . When things got better financially and I didn't need to depend on law, I threw my reading material away." Now he has a CPA who tells him what he needs to know. However, when he needs to do his own reading and research, he knows how to outline and pull out important information (a skill he used in law school). He has self-tailored organizational skills that he developed for himself, and they work well for him.

S1 described himself as a workaholic, at least until three or four years ago. According to him, he liked to work (coming from a work ethic background) and probably worked much too hard. And what has been the effect of learning disabilities? He responded, "Where would I like to be if I didn't have a learning disability? I'm not sure, but I wouldn't like to have accomplished it in exactly the same way I did accomplish it. I think that it may have been a bit easier and less anxiety probably. It may have been a little bit more comfortable in getting there. But I'm sure I wouldn't want to do it the same way with all that anxiety."

S2

S2 has an extremely positive view of his practice of dentistry. He described his work as being very satisfying. In particular, he gets great satisfaction out of doing his work well. He readily explained that he works hard but that he has worked hard his entire life, which probably got him to where he currently stands in life. Ironically, he said, "If things had come easy, maybe I would not be who I am today. I probably wouldn't have stuck with it." When asked if his learning disability affects him professionally, he said he turned what could be routinely looked upon as a minus into a plus. "I do not have much trouble working backward in the dental mirrors. . . . I think that's a real plus. You know, doing intricate work with direct vision is one thing. Doing intricate work through a mirror is something else, and I'm probably pretty good at that. And maybe because I do sometimes see things backward."

Besides being a practicing dentist, S2 also is a clinical professor of dentistry. Part of that role requires writing abilities commensurate with the standards of academic professional publications. He is reluctant to get involved in professional writing. He said that he "knows stuff but finds it difficult to deal with a blank page." At that comment, his wife, who overheard the interview from another room, described how S2's writing was horrendous and dreadful in undergraduate school. He has improved dramatically since being in dental school. From time to time, he edits the professional writing of his wife.

After reflecting on his career choice, S2 concludes it was a good one. In retrospect, the only professions that held any "mystique" were dentistry and medicine. At the same time, he believes he probably could have accomplished any career in which he would have been personally interested. There are exceptions, however. S2 said, "I could have done well in electronics or physics, and I think I could have been a good geologist or teacher or engineer—but I could not have been an English major. People told me to stick to science, and vocational testing confirmed that. So I figured that I better go with my talents. I was not going to try English literature because that would just blow me away, not to mention a foreign language."

He is not surprised he is a dentist because he sees himself having many of the requisite skills. He evaluated his strengths accordingly, stating that he was very good with "abstract reasoning" and spatial relationships. "I can eat those things up, and I don't know why. If it's not visual it's not much trouble because I would miss on visual discrimination. . . . But if you show me something unfolded and say, what would it look like if it were folded, I can tell you what it would look like when you fold it up. . . . I even did well on the chalk carving part of the Dental Aptitude Test so I had what it took to succeed if I could get through the coursework in dental school. I had such a poor academic self-concept."

S3

S3 had a history of work even before she came of age. At the age of ten, she started taking care of children, "almost like a

nanny." This job was done after school and early in the morning.
S3 said, "It got to a point that I was pretty much running a
nursery out of their (parents') home." Child care was an early
endeavor that lasted for several years. At age sixteen, she began
working in a department store. Ultimately, she worked her way
up to manager of a department and began "making good
money." During this time, she became so proficient and effective
in managing her own life that her family gave her more and
more responsibility at home. This started with her doing all of
the food shopping and evolved to a point where she was making
critical decisions for the family.

Upon completing her undergraduate degree, she was employed
as a dormitory counselor and Greek (fraternity and sorority)
advisor at a university that was in her native state but that was
considerably farther from home than the one she attended. This
position allowed her to support herself while getting her master's
degree in counseling. After finishing her master's in one and
one-half years, she took a position as Greek advisor at a public
university in an adjoining state. After attaining experience in
this position, she applied for employment in the student affairs
office at a large urban university in the South (the job she currently holds). She described her job finding process thus: "I did
everything you're not supposed to do on an interview." She did
not feel any pressure to get a job although she did want to leave
her current employment. She related her interview strategy this
way: "This is it, and this is how I am, and you don't have to
like it, but I'm not going to change." She seems to have confidence in this strategy because as she said, "I've never applied
for anything that I didn't get and that I really wanted. I've never
been rejected in that respect and that is more by luck."

It was evident that S3 does not try to hide her learning disabilities when she interviews. This openness is definitely part of
her interviewing strategy. When asked why she does not try to
hide her weaknesses, especially in a position where writing is an
important aspect of the job, she recapitulated her philosophy.

I guess the reason why I do it is because I do not want it to
be a surprise, and I don't want to have to feel dumb in the
process. I want to be up front. I want them to know because

there's no way I can hide it. I cannot unless I dictate, and I do not want to dictate. I can verbally handle it. . . . Even now I write with two-letter words when in an academic setting. If it takes a five-dollar word, I use a two-cent word because I can spell the two-cent word. I can't spell the five-dollar word. Because of that, I don't want down the road not to be thought of as well because of that deficiency. So I smilingly say, "This is it, and if you can't accept this, don't hire me." But I'm not going to put myself in that situation.

She continued to explain, "It's a very quick, very cold, non-discussable issue. I have a learning disability, and my writing skills are not as they should be. I do take a lot of time with that (my learning disability), and I do need to have a secretary that can spell well and who I can work with so that I can do it. . . . And that's just one of my areas. We all have deficits, and this is mine. Then it doesn't become an issue." S3 said that her candid attitude in the interviewing process stems from the notion that "if she doesn't like it, she'll leave" and that "she can always go home."

At the time of the interview, S3 indicated that she had become interested in another job possibility. From all indications, she seems to have a plan for her professional career, yet she has few plans in the personal part of her life. In her words, "My personal life is not quite where I want it to be."

Vocational Summary for Subgroup 1

All members of Subgroup 1 serve in highly professional positions. These positions are similar in that all are "people professions" requiring a great deal of interaction with others. S1 and S3 are highly successful at least in part because of their ability to interact verbally; S2's interaction with clients depends on his ability to inspire trust. All three know how to work with people. Moreover, all three also know how to utilize support systems within their professions. Each has staff personnel who know of their disability and can complement and supplement skills. In order to be effective and successful, Subgroup 1 members need not only personal interaction skills but specific organizational and management skills as well.

Another reason for their vocational success lies in a realistic awareness of how their learning disabilities affect their lives. Through this awareness, they have delineated areas in which they can compensate and other areas in which they need to rely on their support personnel. Assessing and actively working with weaknesses as well as strengths is often the mark of self-confidence. Each of these individuals displays considerable confidence in what he or she can do vocationally.

Success, of course, has strengthened this confidence. Success may also be a factor in another within-group similarity, consistency in employment. All members have remained in their original (chosen) careers and have grown in them. Their stability also attests to the value of being trained specifically for a profession (one could argue that even S3 received training for her present job through her graduate assistantship). All three members have found significant satisfaction through their careers.

Subgroup 2

S4

S4 entered into the world of work several years before the completion of his high school program. He got a job working in a well-established restaurant near his home and over time went from busboy to waiter. This first work experience can only be described as a complete success. He impressed the management and was sought after as a waiter by the restaurant's customers. From his job he received a good income (especially from gratuities), but more importantly, he was able to find vocational success early and used it as an anchor for positive self-esteem. Moreover, he knew that upon graduation from high school he could stay on full-time and make "a very livable wage."

S4 depicted his experience in his first job as one that was very fulfilling. "After I got the system down, it was a piece of cake." At the same time, he always struggled with the spelling of very sophisticated entrées. He disclosed that his own short-hand sufficed until, out of the sight of customers, he would refer back to the spelling in the menu. If he felt he was close in spelling, he would simply gaze over the customer's shoulder to complete his order.

Upon graduation from high school, S4 set his employment sights higher. He wanted to leave his job as a waiter, but he couldn't see himself in a job such as fast food restaurant manager his entire life. He recounted, "I knew I could be somebody, and I wanted to make more than three hundred dollars a week at waiting. . . . My job as waiter meant I would have to work five nights a week, but I saw that as a good job for a kid. Anybody can be a waiter. I wanted to feel better about myself. I wanted to make more money because money means independence."

After completing his training as an electrician, S4 went for an interview at a small company for his first job in his new career. He was offered a job "without any hitches." He also brought up the issue of his learning disability during the interview. His boss didn't really understand his problem, but understood that he wasn't mentally retarded. "I told him up front that when it comes time to write up service tickets, I guess you should know I'm not retarded, I'm not brain damaged, but I have a problem." He explained further, "In everything I do, my learning disability is there, but that isn't any major reason for things not working out." And things have worked out very well for S4 in his job. He has won the admiration of his boss and co-workers for each job he has done. He is well accepted, and learning disabilities are a relatively minor issue in the context of the operation of the company.

Despite his success as an electrician and his adaptation to the world of work, S4 is mindful of how learning disabilities present problems on a daily basis. He readily drew an example of his persisting problems. "Where I'm working, I use two-way radios in trucks. If no radio is available, then I use pay phones. It's nothing for me to pick up the telephone and call my girlfriend and ask her how to spell a word . . . , or I ask my boss." In fact, his boss has been more helpful. S4 stated, "He's been helpful in every way he can. I really appreciate all his help. He went back and changed part names to parts numbers in the computer for me, only to discover it was a better system for the company altogether."

But there are distinct aspects of his job in which S4 is uniquely talented in comparison to his peers. "When my boss, who has worked in the field for years, gets a schematic that's hard to read, he'll ask me to help. I don't know what it is, but as far as blue prints and schematics go, I can master that almost immediately. Sometimes I get lost in a schematic, but I am better than the others." S4 never knew that he had a natural talent for electronics. He can remember taking apart radios when he was in grade school, but never received any encouragement about his "curiosity" from anyone other than his mother.

S4 had determination and perseverance to continue learning on and about his job. "When I reach a problem, I sit down with it, and I am going to get the answer to that problem no matter if I have help or not. When I get it, I go back over it to see how I did it. . . . My nickname at work is Lucky because I'm good at getting things done in the first attempt. They don't realize what I put into it."

S4 is very much aware of his abilities as an elelctrician and aspires to own his own company "like my boss." He views his personality as "not pushy" and believes that he is a fun person to work with. One day he will be his own boss with a good deal of confidence. In his words, "Owning and running my own business, I am not scared of it."

S5

At the time she was interviewed, S5 was not employed because she was staying home with her two young children. Indicative of her spirit, however, she was selling Tupperware out of her house and was gearing up for a busy Christmas season.

Her Tupperware job was her first experience being self-employed. She was always employed after her parents gave her permission to work. In high school, she worked first at a toy store and then for a fast food hamburger chain on weeknights and weekends. She got the job at the hamburger restaurant because "she went to school with the son of the owner." She "enjoyed making money and not being dependent on my parents." After graduating from high school, she began working in a bicycle shop part-time and studied at a local community college.

Her steadiest and most sustained employment was at the daily metropolitan newspaper. She worked for the newspaper for four years and generally described her work experience there as being extremely positive. Because she was one of several family members working at the newspaper, she always felt she had a support system. Her husband and father worked there, and she knew many employees through them.

She did encounter some problems in her work because of her learning disabilities. Writing on the job was a horrific experience, and new learning experiences were difficult. She recalled, "The girl behind me had to proofread my writing. There were even small mistakes like 'wait' for 'want.' She was frustrated with me. I was there four years, and there were things she tried to teach me that I just couldn't get, like the computer. I would often say, 'I have a learning disability; I told you that from the beginning. If I do something wrong, don't yell at me.' But she did yell at me a couple of times. She said, 'I showed you that one thousand times, and you still haven't gotten it!'" S5 reported that she and her co-worker had "basically a friendly relationship, and we still keep it up" (even though she is at home with her children).

Since she has been home with her children, S5 has worked part-time in a large discount department store in the jewelry department. As part of the training for the job, she had to take a courtesy test after watching a training videotape. She scored very well on that test and later was complimented by the owner of the store when he saw her in action. The job was perfect for her "because I had to write sales slips. I was good in math, and I was good in social situations." She gained so much confidence in math she built up the determination to go into accounting.

At the time of the interview, S5 felt she had a full-time job (at home). She was running her household, taking care of her children, managing the finances, and doing some part-time work. She looked forward to going back to work and also wanted to study accounting so she could pursue a permanent career in that field.

S6

The vocational history of S6 is noteworthy because of the un-
usually high number of paying and volunteer jobs he has held
since graduating from high school. Since 1979 (when he returned
to his home city), he has worked in a placement agency (public)
for housing for persons with disabilities, in a typing and filing
position, as a tourist assistant at the New Orleans World Ex-
position, in security for a large oil company, as an assistant for
a national law enforcement association, and as an assistant in
the pet store ("I ran the pet store"). The longest time of consistent employment was six months. Although S6 worked inter-
mittently for a local radio station, performing such jobs as
answering phones, playing commercials, and dubbing tapes, he
did not ultimately find the work satisfying. "I left the radio
station because there weren't any opportunities for me."

S6 has also done much volunteer work for the national, state,
and local spina bifida and learning disabilities associations and
has been an active volunteer for the local Red Cross. In the
Red Cross, he is a volunteer on the Disaster Action Team in the
area of communications. While working with the Red Cross, he
has also become certified in cardiopulminary resuscitation and
first aid.

At the time of the interview, S6 had been in a new job less
than two months. He was delivering fast food products for a
new franchise in a suburban area. This job seems to provide
him with a greater sense of success. He had moved in with his
girlfriend and her two young sons two weeks earlier. It was
readily apparent that he viewed himself as a breadwinner at that
point. He talked about long-term employment with his fast food
employer. He is especially interested in the company plan for
moving up the management hierarchy. Moreover, he enjoys this
job because he "liked driving and didn't want to be locked up
inside all day." He relates his philosophy about his current job
in this manner: "I had a choice, and it's also a challenge. Sometimes I apply for jobs and I know they are going to tell me no,
but I figured it was a challenge. I can do this one."

S6 described some aspects of his job. "I deliver food in a
hot chest contraption about thirty to forty hours a week. I think,

personally, that I do my job well and handle it well. I can handle the public and handle complaints and that kind of stuff. And I think they feel the same way."

S6 related that he has not encountered problems in his jobs emanating from his learning disabilities. "But I'm sure ... if I had difficulty, I could do okay. Because now I know how to accept the fact, if I don't understand good, I'll talk to somebody. And there is a lot of people in this world that are willing to help now than there were back then. My mom looks at it as the Stone Age back when they discovered that I had learning disabilities."

Vocational Summary for Subgroup 2

Subgroup 2 demonstrates many of the same vocational characteristics found in Subgroup 1. The young adults in Subgroup 2 have all discovered compensations and made use of support systems to cope with the demands of the work place successfully. With the same honesty as Subgroup 1, Subgroup 2 members have recognized specific strengths and weaknesses and have used strengths to compensate for weaknesses. An openness about learning disabilities pervades this group. All have revealed their learning disabilities to co-workers and supervisors without any negative repercussions. In fact, this disclosure has had positive effects with employers, who often made appropriate accommodations.

A characteristic that stands out among these three individuals is an easygoing, upbeat, and cheerful attitude. The ability to like and get along with people undoubtedly supports them in the vocational world. The excellent social skills of these adults with learning disabilities enhance their vocational adjustment and success. S4 and S6 explicitly credit their positive outlook and bearing to their struggle with learning disabilities. Somehow these individuals have managed to find strengths within the weaknesses associated with their learning disabilities.

These young adults with learning disabilities aspire to move up the vocational ladder. S4 seems to be moving the most steadily and securely on this path. He has had the most specific job training, the most vocational consistency, and apparently the most vocational success. S5 and S6 lack consistency in their vocational histories, but both reported being at least moderately successful with most employment undertakings. Perhaps the predominant theme from this group is that they are all anticipating future success and satisfaction in the work place.

Subgroup 3

S7

At the time S7 was interviewed for the study, he had been out of work for several months, but he had previously been employed for two and one-half years as a truck driver (pick up and delivery) for a local company. He terminated his employment at the company to travel to Costa Rica with the local church ministry. He did not work after returning to the United States.

His job history starts after leaving high school, when he attended a rehabilitation center to learn auto mechanics. His program focused on academic remedial training plus ceramics and cooking. S7 recounted, "I got bored at that, and then someone told me about construction school in Miami (a five-week course). . . . But after I graduated, I found out that the school wasn't a reputable place. . . . I wasn't able to get hired."

He stayed in Florida and did manual labor for two or three months and then returned home. He got a job with the Louisiana Roads Department but then went back to Florida to work on the roads there. After one week, he returned home. He then got his truck driving job and worked for five consecutive years,[1] but he doesn't want to return to truck driving. As he stated, "There is not much thought to driving a truck. After five years, I guess I achieved as far as I could go with them (his company), and I got involved in my church, and they were more worldly and educated about what's right and wrong. The job didn't appeal to me then."

S7 then tried to learn cabinet making at a local vocational-

---

1. While S7's accounting of two and one-half years of truck driving and five years of consecutive employment do not logically compute, this is the information obtained by the authors.

technical school. That training program did not work out as he thought. This was the last time he tried to seek out vocational training opportunities.

When he was working, S7 related that his learning disabilities created problems for him. He had problems reading the delivery ticket and making sure the order was correct. It took him a while to learn his routes, but he knew them perfectly after a half year. Reading a map and translating the information for travel was also difficult. It was not uncommon for him to get mixed up, but he always persevered. He conceded that his perseverance came from the awareness that "there were too many things I couldn't do, and this was a nonunion job in which I had a chance to succeed."

S7 thinks that a major issue in his employment was his peer relations. At first, he was accepted by his co-workers, who seemed to like him. As time wore on, however, S7 found he had little in common with his co-workers and eventually felt like a social outcast. "They . . . were in their own world. They liked the girls and the gambling and all the drinking and all that stuff. And I didn't care for that. . . . They're always in debt and needing money, and I had all my money."

Despite being unemployed, S7 did not have a plan to gain employment at the time of the interview. Moreover, he does not have any plans to attend any vocational programs found in his community. He does have a tentative goal of completing his GED but has not explored the logistics of getting into a GED program.

S8

S8 began in the world of work as a helper in a family-owned restaurant. She began working there after a failure experience in her first job out of secondary school. In that experience, she worked briefly at an exercise center, but "didn't have confidence and was too nervous." She remembered, "I had to write down how much this person weighed and if they were doing good. But I couldn't really spell well or measure the weight."

To a great extent, her family salvaged her from issues of low self-esteem and a deep lack of confidence by immediately putting her to work. She brought food and bussed dishes. She did not write down food orders but did write some drink orders. She felt good about her abilities. She recalled, "I used my own code. Sometimes I couldn't read it, but mostly I could. But I had to memorize my own code."

Her job enabled her to make money, which she enjoyed spending. Not only did her job afford her a degree of independence, but she also used it for socialization purposes. She often went to bars with her fellow co-workers after the restaurant closed. All in all, the social and vocational experiences she encountered were devoid of any problems stemming from her learning disabilities. Feeling free of learning disabilities reinforced her feeling of accomplishment.

Her job also gave her confidence to pursue her GED. From the money she earned, she paid for tutoring for her GED preparatory lessons. Unfortunately, the tutoring did not help. S8 became very frustrated and scrapped the goal to achieve her GED.

At that point, she decided she would try another job and left the family's restaurant. She got a job as a dental assistant on a tip from her GED tutor. At first, she was intimidated with the writing that had to be done as part of her job, but her boss was very understanding and very accommodating. In time, she did well, but she also began to yearn for greater challenges. S8 elaborated, "After a couple years of the same thing, I knew I had to do something else. I had to try to learn something else because I just didn't want to be stuck in that even though it was good for me." She related further, "I felt good about my performance because I was reliable in my work, and I did well in handling instruments, cleaning instruments, cleaning the office, talking to patients, answering the phone, and billing. Collecting money was most difficult if I was not given the exact amount. I learned to use the VISA machine, which helped. I really liked that, eventually, even though at first it seemed very hard."

In retrospect, it was her work in the family restaurant she thought was the most challenging. Admittedly, it was not beyond her limits, but she asserted that she created her own challenges. "Creating my own code, talking to customers eye-to-eye, laughing and joking was my challenge." As much as she felt challenged at the restaurant, her work at the dentist office gave her a clear sense of career.

At the time of the interview, S8 was working part-time as a child care worker. She had considered other careers because she "didn't want to feel trapped." Moreover, she felt that her jobs in the family restaurant and the dentist's office were given to her and not things for which she had worked. She felt secure in being supported by her husband but felt she could always get a job on her own. She revealed that she had applied and gotten a dental job on her own, but didn't take it because of low pay and long hours. She simply stated, "It just wasn't worth it."

She has decided to continue looking for work and hopes to be able to apply the typing skills she acquired from a community college program. It is her desire that she will get a job doing light typing, copying, and word processing. She admittedly has no big dreams but wants to work in a job where she can get raises and vacations. She did know that she "wanted to do something else" (something quite different from what she had done in the past). She has no illusions about her own skills. "It's hard times finding a job around here. Especially for me, because I can't do much in secretarial work or anything like that."

S9

At the age of twenty-two, S9 was the youngest adult with learning disabilities interviewed. To some extent, it was difficult to discern a pattern of employment and vocational issues. Yet, some interesting insights were given in the interview.

At the time of the interview, S9 had been working in a gas station for only a few days. Already he was encountering problems on the job. He explained how his problems with numbers "got in the way." "I have tried checking the pumps and writing the numbers down. Every time I see a number and I don't think about it, I'll say it backward or something. That's money! Also, someone might ask me the time and I'll tell it backward, like 5:03 is 5:30. They'll look at me like I am a freak or something. It happens all the time, on license plates and credit cards. It also happens with words—everything." S9 receives commission on what he can sell at the gas station. He also gets tips. The most money is in selling auto parts, but S9 doesn't like to do that. He revealed, "I just can't get the nerve to tell an old lady that she needs a filter, etc. They tell me the more you sell the better you do, but I can't do that."

There have been numerous jobs in S9's short time in the world of work. He worked in an auto body shop part-time and worked as a plumber's helper. His assessment of his work as a plumber's helper was, "I was good but not fast enough." He worked as a helper in a bridal shop as a stock boy. He was also a carpenter's helper and sought employment in a plant shop.

An issue in his work (as earlier mentioned) is S9's slowness. S9 is painfully aware of his problem: "Every job I have, I put pride into it. And I figure I did a good job and the guy says, 'You took so long!' Like, okay man. And I'm sitting here trying to be perfect and he says, 'You're taking too long doing it.' And I have been taken off the jobs. I'll be doing something great, but I'll be doing it too slow."

It was quite evident that slowness as well as forgetfulness were issues in most of his jobs, but these problems especially stood out in his mechanical jobs. S9 related, "Mechanic work is not too good a job for me to be in. . . . You read a work order, and you have to remember everything on it, everything to do. . . . So many things to do that I'd leave a few things and forget them and not even know they were there. And somebody would say, 'What about this?' Pressure is, like, work orders."

S9 is adamant about not revealing his learning disabilities to his co-workers or his supervisors. In all his jobs, he never told anyone. Part of his motivation is hiding his problems. The other part is his inability to explain his problems adequately. He said, "If I did say something, then they would ask me all kinds of questions and all kinds of details, and I would never be able to answer them. So I just don't let them know."

His lack of direction has caused problems. His mother tries to help him with career decisions and has cried because her son did not have a job. She has told S9, "If it wasn't for me, you would be dead," the truth of which S9 implicitly admits.

S9 also does not like looking for jobs. He thinks that filling out applications is a waste of time and doesn't like to go to interviews. He also hates to keep calling about jobs "because they get sick of me calling. So I blow it off." He says, "I get worked up over thinking I'd get a job and when it doesn't happen, I get depressed."

Vocational Summary for Subgroup 3

If Subgroups 1 and 2 share a number of vocational characteristics, Subgroup 3 presents the other end of the spectrum of vocational characteristics. Rather than a history of success, the members of Subgroup 3 have accumulated a track record of mostly failure in jobs. Because of these frustrating and negative experiences with work, they are apprehensive about the future. As a group, these individuals do not seem sure of how they can contribute to society vocationally or how they will be able to compete in terms of socioeconomic status. It is not surprising that these adults lack a great deal of self-confidence in vocational skills and abilities, including the critical skill of getting along with others on the job. They are sometimes victims of their own failures in that they have difficulty reentering the job market after leaving or losing previous jobs.

The lack of vocational success bears a relation to the dependent adult lifestyles of the members of Subgroup 3. They are forced to be dependent on a parent or a spouse because they have so much difficulty supporting themselves. In addition, a predilection to dependency may also foster vocational difficulties. None has real aspirations of success in the job market. They have had so little experience with success they have no idea of how to become successful. These individuals tend to be vague about where they should be on the vocational track. They do not plan to go back to school for further training. The attainment of a GED may indirectly relate to vocational aspirations, but no one in this group had actual plans for use of the GED. The chances for vocational success and satisfaction appear rather limited for Subgroup 3.

Vocational Summary across All Subgroups

One of the more important observations is the similarity of Subgroups 1 and 2 and the contrast between those subgroups and Subgroup 3. Six adults with learning disabilities in this study have experienced varying degrees of vocational success. All six have learned to compensate for their disabilities in order to achieve. They have accepted their disabilities and have not lost confidence in themselves. All these individuals are comfortable with their learning disabilities in work situations. The members of Subgroup 3 have not experienced the same degree of adaptation, however. Their potential for change is limited. Their own awareness of the specific nature of their disability is greatly lacking compared to the other subgroups.

All nine adults struggle with their unique learning disabilities every day. There are times when the disability has little effect or relevance, but anyone in the study may have to face the challenges imposed by the disability at any given moment. All carry strong memories of having struggled in the past. Subgroups 1 and 2 make better use of those memories. For all the adults in this study, vocational success seems to correlate with personal happiness and satisfaction. All the adults with learning disabilities who have had vocational success have found self-worth through their achievement. The three less successful adults may be missing this essential ingredient that often contributes to a healthy self-concept.

CHAPTER 5

Social/Emotional

Subgroup 1

S1

One might expect an individual of such professional stature to exude self-confidence and ability. Even though S1 is aware of his success and is comfortable in his surroundings, his accomplishments seemed discordant with development during childhood. In his younger years, his self-esteem was low. He was "physically small, somewhat protected, bashful, and shy." Elementary school was difficult and frustrating. His parents expected him to excel. Nevertheless, he felt that he received a great deal of support at home. He said he was a "good kid." During his years in high school, the teaching brothers gave him "tremendous encouragement." He began to develop "a lot of self-esteem." He participated in extracurricular activities such as drama and became a school leader. He did well academically, which required five to six hours of studying every day. "Notwithstanding, it was practically killing me."

S1 made insightful reflections on the effect his successful but arduous experiences had upon his social development. Because of his learning difficulties, he devoted much more time than his peers to studying. His determination to do well paid off "in a lot of respects. There've been some negative by-products. Although I did get involved in a lot of extracurricular activities through high school, I think that because I spent so much time on my studies, I had less time to spend in the development of social graces, less time to develop just hanging out, if you will, with the boys and the girls. So I feel like maybe I missed out on the development of some social graces or some social opportunities. Same thing through college. So although, yes, there were some positive things, I missed out on part of living."

This perceived lack of social development has had a significant impact on his adult life. It has altered his expectations for his youngest son, who is classified as having learning disabilities. "That's why in working with (my son), yes, it's important to have him study, work at becoming determined, and so forth. But I can see now that equally as important is being able to develop the social graces, being able to interact with his peer group. And that's part of living and part of growing up, just as much, if not more, than the book work."

S1 also sees that his time in high school has affected how he acts socially as an adult. He said that it's difficult for him to get close to social acquaintances. In fact, he prefers to keep a distance. "I missed out in high school on a lot of social opportunities, and I'm not interested, or afraid to tackle, or I don't want to have anything to do with, certain similar social activities now. Has it impacted my life even to this day? Yeah, no question about the fact, in my mind, that it's helped mold my profile of social activity."

S1 has not forgotton that prior to his success in high school, college, and the legal and business worlds, he often felt that he was not a particularly capable person. In many ways, his drive and determination represent an attempt to compensate or even overcompensate for feelings of inferiority. He referred a number of times to the pain he experienced as a child. He reflected that "there're a lot of remnants. I guess maybe remnants of scar tissue from earlier years forever." What exactly is this scar tissue? "The feelings of inferiority when I was a youngster, feelings of feeling like a little kid. I'm bigger than that now in that I know I'm not a little kid now, but—I don't know what it is—there's a certain quality of regressing back every once in awhile. There's a certain phenomenon or regression. So I am what I am, not only what I am now, but I am what I have been for fifty-six years."

Certain types of social situations cause discernible anxiety for S1. He feels that some of his fears are connected to childhood insecurities. As an adult, he has learned to cope using skills that may have developed in high school and beyond. He feels uncomfortable in large social gatherings, but a "certain amount of ham in me" can rise to the occasion.

S1 possesses both a drive to succeed in whatever he does and an ability to act out social scripts successfully. This combination of traits allows him to cope with the social and business situations that make him uncomfortable. "Even in those circumstances where I would tend to be anxious, I could always put on whatever coat of armor was needed to be put on and go into the fray, knowing that I could win the battle if I fought hard enough. And that's been sort of my approach. Even when I put on my tuxedo, and I've got to go to a large social gathering, I put on my 'Hamlet disguise,' and I'll play the play like anybody else."

S1 does not believe that such anxiety in dealing with large groups is completely normal. "There's no need for a man fifty-six years of age to walk into a social gathering and feel uncomfortable, and yet I do. I cope with it. I play the play and so forth."

Another method of coping is actively seeking situations in which he can most easily feel comfortable. He purposely became involved in a small, seven-person firm. He asserted that he would not be able to practice in a large law firm. "I would find all those attorneys who are constantly competing and interacting with each other on a day-in-day-out basis. I would find that pretty much threatening."

S1 has also chosen a social life that focuses on a few close friendships. He and his wife are "not social gadabouts." They entertain at home with dinners and small parties. Their swimming pool is often a center of small social gatherings with friends and family. "We have some very good friends, and we cherish our friends, and we like to be with them." S1 added that he spends time with just the other husbands on occasions. He and his wife often vacation with this circle of close friends. S1 does belong to large social groups, almost a requirement for an established professional in the Mardi Gras culture of New Orleans. He reiterated his feelings about his involvement in these social activities. "I find that I'm a lot more comfortable with those close friends. I find myself a lot less comfortable in large groups, what we would call social command performances."

S1 feels most comfortable in professional situations when he is problem solving in his own specialty of expertise. When asked about his most comfortable social circumstances, he responded,

"Very, very often it is when I'm alone. I'm an alone person. I like to do things alone. Saturday in the office alone is an extremely productive, comfortable time for me. At home, during the week, I'll take off a day from the office when I know no one is at home, and I'll use the time to make telephone calls or use the time to think and to plan. I use the time to get out in the backyard and piddle in the garden. I use the time to get in the kitchen and cook. I like my alone times." He enjoys unstructured time. It is not unusual for him to have several projects going at one time. He likes to get back to each one, but he does not feel compelled to finish all of them.

S1's comfort with "alone times" is consistent with the impression that he is largely a private person. He has the social skills to deal with a wide variety of people but chooses to maintain a certain distance. "Up to a point, I can make friends easily. I'm not the type of person that wants to get too intimate with people." He does feel close to his small circle of good friends and is "reasonably intimate" with them. He is very conscious of distinguishing social acquaintances. "I don't think I tend to be too transparent. I think I can get along with them," but he only opens up to friends that he's "not threatened by."

S1 learned to cope in adult life with learning disabilities through "overpreparation" and making use of "available resources." These two methods became his "formula for success." In more recent years, however, he has wondered if his drive took a toll on him emotionally. Throughout his career, he tried to read everything necessary and to keep up with all his professional responsibilities. As a result, "I was constantly anxious, and I was constantly under the gun because there were a lot of things that I had to read." As he became more independently successful through investments, he realized that he didn't need to depend on law. At present, he tries to do less himself, relies more on others to do work that is taxing on him, and is generally much more relaxed as a result. Success taught S1 that he didn't have to do everything himself. He works less but enjoys it more.

S2

It was easy to agree with S2's self-appraisal that he had come a long way since second or third grade. This easygoing, successful dentist had spent much of his life as a child struggling to understand why he saw the world differently from other kids. A memorable and significant experience in S2's childhood was the moment he was able to interpret the visual information of a picture into a meaningful whole. "That's when I realized something was wrong. Other people could appreciate these things and I couldn't." He stated that at that time, in second grade, he was too young for an "emotional reaction," but he added that he felt depressed that other kids could read and understand things on a page, but he had "no idea of what was going on."

Specific difficulties with visual language (ie., reading, spelling, and writing) impeded success in the classroom for most of S2's youth. The frustration and hurt from continual academic problems were exacerbated because S2's family clearly felt he ought to do well at school. "It was still pretty bad, even until I got into college."

S2 seems to have experienced some emotional difficulties stemming from low self-esteem. In contrast, he remembered his social life as pretty satisfactory throughout his childhood and into the present. He depicted his relationships at school with peers and adults as "pretty typical. I think I got along pretty well with other kids." By the time he was in high school, he had a circle of friends and was passing through the normal ups and downs of adolescence. His wife proudly pointed out that "in high school, this man was a social butterfly. He dated extensively." S2 mentioned that he knew and socialized with many people in high school.

Learning problems continued to affect his performance with school work, but throughout high school he became more adaptive to academic demands. He worked diligently and acquired a degree of perseverance that far exceeded that of his peers. His formidable persistence paid off, and he was accepted to the flagship university of the state. Although S2 acknowledged he succeeded in high school largely through tenacity, he was more likely during that time to undercut the reasons for his success. S2 had always felt that he was "street smart," but he reasoned that he had "conned" his way through school.

By the time he began his studies at the university, S2 still doubted his own intellectual skills. A significant change of attitude began to occur in college after he started dating the woman whom he eventually married. His wife, a speech pathology major, sensed that S2 had learning disabilities. She informed him of the term and let him know that other people experienced similar problems. "She would talk about these interesting things and I'd say, 'Hey, that applies to me.' Or I would say, 'I do this,' and she'd say, 'Yeah, you're LD.'" S2 had always believed that his problems were unique and personal. He recalled, "Before that, I knew there was . . . something different, but . . . I didn't have anything to blame. It was just there, and I didn't know about it." This new awareness helped him achieve a more positive image of himself. "It made me think that for the first time the world wasn't just divided up into smart people and dumb people and that I wasn't on the dumb side."

S2 does not think that learning disabilities affected his social life in either school or adulthood. He has an active family life. Many activities such as picnics, school functions, and the PTA revolve around the kids, but he occasionally has time to go out with friends and colleagues to dinner, shows, and seafood picnics, and to take advantage of many of the social opportunities readily found in New Orleans. S2 summed up his sense of the present with his characteristic wit by saying he had a "reasonably good social life . . . for a married man." In these situations, having learning disabilities is not an issue. S2 doesn't have to be concerned with hiding his learning disabilities because it simply doesn't come up in social interactions. No one would have reason to question his learning abilities or infer that he has learning disabilities. Additionally, S2 feels that his ability to read body language helps him negotiate social situations.

Upon reflection, S2 was able to delineate specific social occasions when his learning disabilities seemed to be a factor. He said that he sometimes finds large groups a little overpowering. In particular, the possibility of having to read aloud presents a social situation in which his learning disabilities might become apparent. "If I had to get up in front of a group and read something that I did not get a chance to go over, that would be very anxious—getting back to the LD." He is not embarrassed to read in front of his wife, but he expressed concern that his difficulty with reading belies the image of a professional and

successful man. People would question his abilities as a dentist
if he indicated that he had trouble reading because "a doctor
should know these things."

Being able to relieve stress acts as an adaptive feature of S2's
adult life. He says he is "least anxious when I'm fishing or
gardening."

When asked to describe himself emotionally, S2 responded,
"Apprehension, nervousness, . . . careful, . . . I try to be pretty
cautious, tend not to take big risks." He feels that his tendency
to be cautious is a factor for success professionally. He also
stated that he is perceived as being fair-minded because he will
wait to comment on something until he has given it some
thought. But he added that his "deliberate" approach was partially an adaptive response to learning disabilities. "I want to
make sure that I'm understanding things really the way they are
because I do realize I sometimes don't see things really as they
are, and I want to make sure I do. I guess some people take
that as being kind of a stuffed shirt at times, but it's just the
way I have to be."

S2 appears to have accepted the 'way he has to be.' He
reported that he has a very healthy self-esteem as an adult. "I'd
say I think a lot of myself. I don't feel like I'm the very best,
but certainly not the least or less than the majority. . . . I see an
awful lot of other people, and I don't have any problems with
my self-esteem." He sees himself as more successful than others.

This strong self-concept stems from recent critical incidents
as well as building blocks of success from his past. According
to his wife, S2 only recently gained a more positive sense of his
own intelligence through taking a graduate course. When he did
better than a smart friend, "it finally convinced him that it
wasn't just a matter of being street smart, that he really had
good analytical skills and that he was really bright."

S2's demeanor is quiet and calm. From outward appearances,
he would not be considered "high strung." "I don't think I'm
excessively anxious. Normal things make me anxious." S2 described his most stressful activity as an experience most people
fear only from the patient's perspective. "Most anxious has to
be when I'm giving an injection," and he hastened to say that
he hasn't had a problem yet. S2 is also concerned about hurting

others emotionally. He invoked a dental metaphor to state, "It's not socially acceptable to stick pins in people."

S3

S3 had some difficulty remembering many events prior to seventh grade. She did relate that she spent much time with younger children. The experiences of one summer especially gave her opportunities to have leadership roles with younger children. "Most of my friends were gone, and that was when I played with a lot younger kids in the summer . . . , which gave me that ability to be head of a group because I was the oldest." S3 had brought up the same theme earlier in the interview: "I had a lot of friends as I was growing up. I became the leader because that was one of the things I could master very well." Sometimes being the most grown-up kid in the group wasn't so great. Another memory from childhood recalled a particularly difficult summer. "I learned to swim when I was eight. And I was the oldest kid learning to swim. My mother would drag me out of bed at seven o'clock and dump me in this freezing cold water. I hated it and still don't know how to swim very well because of it. It was one of those negative experiences that continued."

S3's almost heated response(s) seemed to evoke a sense of rebelliousness from her childhood that she could still feel. "I was very much a rebel and very deviant in a lot of ways. I started smoking in sixth grade. I got kicked out of every school. I did it just because I didn't like their policy. I thought it was stupid, or I wanted to make trouble. And did it quite well. Because of that, I became the leader of my social crowd. And as I grew older, I still had that kind of thing with people. I intimidated people a lot faster than I would like to. I don't mean to, but I have a tendency to do that. As I get older, I'm more conscious of it and catch it faster."

In the seventh grade, S3 was formally diagnosed as having learning disabilities. The explicit recognition of her disability affected most of her adolescence, particularly in respect to personal relationships. Her parents acknowledged that she wasn't "just pretending to be dumb" and arranged for her to work with tutors. Her favorite tutor gave her academic survival skills in a way that was comfortable. "I always remember spending time doing work for my tutor, but I don't remember doing school work." Her tutor helped her develop her sight memory. At the present time, S3 teaches a course on study skills, one reflection of the tutor's influence.

The effect of learning disabilities on her relationships with her tutor, family members, and friends was soon compounded by another significant variable. At thirteen, S3 experienced an ordeal that had a profound effect upon her socially and emotionally. She was diagnosed as sterile, and the trauma was exacerbated as soon as she returned from the doctor's office.

As we were driving up into my driveway, there was my next-door neighbor standing out (who asked) "What's the news?" And I said to my mother, "Do not tell her. Just don't say anything. Just say you don't know anything." And we had found out that I was sterile, or so they thought. I found out just two years ago I wasn't. At thirteen, when all I thought about as all children do, playing with dolls and having a family and everything, that was shattered for me. I wasn't real comfortable with having that shared with anyone. And my mother gets out of the car and out comes Mrs. B., "What did the doctor say?" Before I knew anything, my mother was like verbal diarrhea, and it all came out. Part of that was my mother's own need to come to terms with it directly for herself. At age thirteen, I refused to believe that that could be the possibility. At that point in time, my relationship with my family changed significantly. And it wasn't until about three years ago that I explained that to my mother and why I've never trusted her since, and I don't trust many other people since.

But S3 did learn to trust some other people during this time, and in a way, the learning disabilities provided an impetus to build trusting relationships. She was depressed and tried to commit suicide. The tutoring sessions began to resemble "mini-counseling." S3 learned to turn to her tutor for emotional needs because the learning disabilities had helped develop a sense of intimacy between them. "She was basically the only person that

I did trust. And as I did that, my tensions would diminish. She helped in some of those respects of just giving me games to do that. Just the fact that I would say I was studying was good for my mother. And it would be games that she drew from the game book (used in tutoring)."

Both the tutor and the psychologist who had diagnosed the learning disabilities suggested that S3's father work with her on learning games at home. "Because my mother couldn't deal with it, my father would have to. That caused some marital problems in my family. I didn't really know at the time," she elaborated. Although she had stated that "neither of my parents accepted the problem," she also said her relationship with her father deepened through the time they spent together. They often worked on jigsaw puzzles together. In addition to being helpful for analytical and visual-perceptual skills, working on jigsaw puzzles gave them a chance to interact socially, something the psychologist had recommended. "That helped change my life and grow closer to my father. . . . We spent many hours alone in the living room, doing jigsaw puzzles, talking."

Emotional support in her family also came from an uncle who spent a great deal of time in the home. She remembers fondly that he showed her games and card tricks. She felt loved. This closeness helped her keep frustrations about learning disabilities in perspective. "So there was a lot of family social time that I spent. So school just wasn't that important because other things were. So I never really lost that sense of confidence in myself."

Whereas these relationships helped foster self-esteem and trust, her relationships with her mother and sister were not as close. S3 only mentioned her sister once, saying they didn't get along. Her mother did not offer much support for coping with the two critical issues of her adolescence, sterility and learning disabilities. S3 stated that much of her independence was a natural result of trust betrayed. "When I was thirteen, when I had that experience with my mother, it was one of those things that, 'I'd better rely on myself. If I want to get anything, I'd better go out and get it.'" These negative aspects of her family life left her with ambivalent feelings about her mother but also were at least partially responsible for her formidable drive.

These two critical issues also affected her peer relationships. She had had experience taking care of children starting at age ten. She worked even more with young children when she discovered she was sterile. She feels that it was a "vicarious experience." She worked early in the morning and after school and "was pretty much running a nursery out of their (parents') home." She did have many friends in high school, but almost all had some characteristic that kept them out of the mainstream. One was overweight; another was artistic; S3 was sterile and learning disabled. "We all had different handicaps. We all had our own idiosyncracies . . . It just worked out fine." They always had a lot a fun socially, but S3 never felt really close.

She did share more with the girlfriend who was overweight. They would talk, commiserate, and discuss their feelings with a seriousness often associated with adults. "As very young children, we were talking very grown-up things." They also swore a lot. On occasion, S3 would get into trouble at school. "I always stood up to authority. All my friends thought that was very cool." She ran afoul of the dress code and fought for women's rights, but didn't interact very much with boys. She had already decided that her sterility made it useless.

Toward the end of high school, S3 began to assert her independence. She worked at paying jobs after school and during the summer. She smoked. She drank. "I started making critical decisions in the family. And I played very much an adult role, and my parents played, to some degree, very much a child role. It wasn't 'Give me advice' or that kind of thing. It was me doing the opposite of feminine and still is to this day. And as a result of that, I needed to get away. They were driving me crazy. And the only way, I thought, was how everyone else was doing it, was to go to college. And in my neighborhood, that was the thing to do. You just went to college." She felt that her parents were overly dependent on her, and the opportunity to leave home was highly motivating. "I wasn't thinking of going to college for education. I was going to college to get away from my parents."

S3 set high expectations for herself. "I went to college, and I was determined to succeed. And I was not going to go back." But choosing the "right" college where she'd be able to be successful required a special strategy. She set her sights on a college where the academic standards would not be demanding. Her difficulties with directions and spatial orientation caused additional concern. She needed a relatively small school where she'd be able to get around comfortably. Additionally, it was important not to be too far from home. A second-line university fit these requirements and was the only college to which she applied.

When she first began at the university, her mother would call her every night and beg her to come home. Coping with both parental and academic pressure, as well as adjusting to a new life, tested her determination to make it in college. "I had an overwhelming sense of responsibility. My freshman year was a terrible experience. I started drinking senior year in high school, and the worst of it was my freshman year in college."

One reason that she did get through college was the ability to apply study skills she had picked up through her tutoring. At least equally important, she found a professor who was sensitive to the needs of students with learning disabilities and recognized S3's talents and intellectual abilities. "It helped that I had Dr. L. in most of my classes. She was basically an LD specialist. She was my primary advisor, and that really helped because she knew about my past."

In courses where she had to do a great deal of writing, her grades suffered. "I realized that the grades were the depressing part of college." To cope, she chose academic areas that interested her but placed less demands on her writing skills. "I mean, I wasn't dumb. I took courses that would be successful." Eventually, she started getting "B's." For the first time in her life, it was not "horrendous" to show her report card to her parents.

In the last semester of senior year, S3 was referred for the "Greek advisor" position at another university in the state. She accepted the job, which required her to enroll as a graduate assistant. Graduate school proved to be less difficult than undergraduate. S3 became increasingly aware of her intellectual talents. She did require extensions for papers, but she planned her time accordingly. "I guess I never thought that I was that much different. I never compared if I studied harder than any-body else." Instead, she was confident that her study skills would produce the results she expected.

In her present social life, S3 is aware that her difficulties with reading and spelling can make her uncomfortable. She clearly identified writing as the most anxiety-producing aspect of her adult life. Difficulties with writing require her to organize her social life in special ways. She doesn't write birthday cards or thank-you letters, but uses equally acceptable (albeit more costly) methods of taking a friend out for a birthday dinner or making phone calls to say thank-you. She chooses her grocery store carefully, mainly for the purpose of writing a check without embarrassment. "I don't go to Schwegmann's (supermarket) be-cause I don't know how to spell it." Instead, she chooses a store where the name is visible when she is at the register.

S3 feels that she is not consciously aware of other effects on her social life. "I've never thought my learning disability affected any other part of my life other than reading. And I very much compartmentalized it in that respect." With a little more thought, she added that learning disabilities *must* affect how she deals with people, especially because of the demands she puts upon herself in dealing with learning disabilities. "My demands are high on me because I refuse to let myself fail. And I refuse to admit that I have a problem. I know I have a problem, and I acknowledge it. I like definition, and sometimes my friendships and my relationships don't have that, and I feel very uncom-fortable with those simply because I like rights and wrongs." These remarks provided some insight into S3's relationships with other people. "I think that I make friends easily, but I think that my demands on how I anticipate a friend to be are too high. I have very strong demands on myself, and I expect that. And I always get disappointed. And that's happened as a child." Furthermore, making friendships runs the risk of "rejection. I just can't deal with it. So I don't. It's like writing is hard, so I try to avoid it."

S3 views herself as a private person who spends a great deal of time alone. She doesn't particularly enjoy large social gatherings. She feels she is adept at mingling with a crowd, but she is more comfortable if she maintains a sense of distance. "I guess I've learned pretty much just all along to rely just on me. Whenever I've gotten close to somebody, I've normally gotten hurt. And there's very few people that I trust. And even when I've had an intimate relationship with someone, I've had a very standoffish approach."

When S3 does get close to someone, she tends to choose individuals older than herself. "I'm much more comfortable with people much older than me. Chronologically, I'm only twenty-six, but where I am in every other part of my life is much older. I'm attracted to much older sexual partners. I'm attracted to much older friendships and that kind of thing."

Many of S3's social and emotional concerns could be construed as directly affected by learning disabilities. Undoubtedly, her present life bears the impress of a constellation of past experiences as well as the daily struggles that she incurs because of learning disabilities. Yet, the learning disabilities do occasionally act as an impetus to becoming a socially successful individual. At her sixteenth birthday, she was terribly upset about receiving a book she was incapable of reading. She vowed to become a voracious reader and in the last two years has read four hundred books. This achievement made her realize how much the learning disabilities had deprived her socially. That realization became clear when she recently visited her family at Christmas. "For the first time in my life, we had a conversation about books we had read. It was one of those things where I felt like 'I'm really in society. I can talk about a book!'" Now, she has her sights on a Ph.D. to fulfill a lingering ambition to be a scholar.

S3 is a complex individual, replete with contradictions, but contradictions that attest to an emotional honesty. Clearly, having learning disabilities has a daily impact on her sense of self. She pursues her ambitions actively and toughly, and some of that toughness might be a response to the obstacles and the hurt she has faced. Her own insight may appear incongruous with specific incidents but does offer the most parsimonious explanation of how an individual emotionally copes with learning disabilities: "I'm real comfortable with it and have been all along."

Social/Emotional Summary for Subgroup 1

Fewer similarities exist in the social/emotional domain as compared to education and vocation for Subgroup 1. All members of the subgroup are rated as moderately to highly adapted in social/emotional aspects of adult life, yet each adaptation is unique. All members expressed some equivocal attitudes about their degree of satisfaction. It is within this equivocation that differences are most pronounced.

S1 seems to have the most active formal social life. He qualified this status by stating that he is not entirely comfortable with his social life. He equated many social activities with "performing" and attributed much of his discomfort to a lack of "social graces" that he may not have acquired because of the limitations imposed by learning disabilities. S2 does not feel that learning disabilities deterred social development in high school and college. Nevertheless, his present social activities are somewhat restricted (e.g., he can not maintain written correspondence), and he shies away from situations that might expose his learning disability. S3 believes that her social development was aberrant due to learning disabilities as well as other factors. Rated slightly lower in her overall adaptation than S1 and S2, she sees some negative repercussions in adult life, especially in "trust" issues.

The common element within the subgroup seems to be a social life that has suffered because of the effects of learning disabilities. S1 and S2 explicitly depicted themselves as "alone people," and S3 certainly has boundaries and barriers to the outside. All are careful about relationships. All subjects stated that they do not feel comfortable in large crowds. All these characteristics probably are shared by most nondisabled persons, yet in one way or another, these adults all feel they have been forced by learning disabilities to develop specific adaptive mechanisms. This limitation had affected both emotional and social satisfaction.

Subgroup 2

S4

S4 had difficult social experiences while growing up, largely because he moved around the public school system so frequently before finally finding success at a private clinical high school for students with learning disabilities. The constant disruption of switching from school to school at times precluded social experiences such as making close friends. Additionally, the inability of teachers and parents to understand why spelling and reading were so difficult for him led to experiences that were trying socially and emotionally. At one point in elementary school, he was placed in a class for students with mental retardation. He survived emotionally through a strong self-concept that remained secure in a situation surely threatening to many people. S4 was able to cope with being placed in a class for students with mental retardation by believing in himself despite the message he had received from the school system. Luckily, the teacher immediately recognized that S4 was not retarded, and after two weeks, S4 was moved out of the class. He can understand why he wound up in such a circumstance, but the experience still hurt. "It was disturbing. But at the time, that's what my mom thought was right."

Much of S4's public school experiences accentuated feelings of being different from other kids. He reflected that in school, "they isolate you, make you feel like something's wrong with you." In many ways, most of his classes tended to emphasize his problems with spelling and reading, but he resisted developing a negative attitude about himself. "You can sit there and dwell on your faults for the rest of your life and wind up being an old person in a one-room shack living off the government, or you can just overlook it."

The general lack of knowledge about learning disabilities when he was in elementary school seemed to affect S4 adversely, at least until he went to the high school for students with learning disabilities. Before the term learning disabilities became generally understood, "you were either one of two ways, either normal or retarded," he said. As a result, he often felt socially isolated because he was different. He recounted that "when you're young and still in school, people say, 'Oh, stay away from him, son. There's something wrong with him.'"

From descriptions of his childhood, S4 must have had some special qualities to have coped and emerged with such an apparently strong and positive self-concept. He was able to identify several characteristics that enabled him to survive emotionally and socially. He stated that he was able to get through bad times by relying on his sense of humor. He can make people laugh, to some extent because he's not afraid to laugh at himself. "My way of dealing with it is to laugh about it, and not only my laughing about it but to make everybody else laugh about it." Being able to laugh at himself reflects a kind of self-confidence or positive self-esteem. "I can definitely laugh at myself. I think I'm the funniest person I know."

He was able to withstand the failures in public shoool through specific emotional coping mechanisms. S4 stated that he coped emotionally with school difficulties and failure through a process of not investing himself emotionally in his specific academic problems at school. In other words, his self-concept was strong enough that he was able to separate his sense of self from how he performed in specific situations.

S4 mentioned other characteristics that helped him cope with the impact of learning disabilities in his childhood as well as in adulthood. He sees himself as a very persistent person who "won't give up." His persistence is realistic. When help is warranted, he's not afraid to ask for assistance. He also achieved significant success as a target shooter starting when he was nine and continuing through high school. He was able to capitalize on this success and to build a self-concept largely resilient to negative educational experiences.

His parents were a source of support as he was growing up. They told him he *wasn't* retarded when he was placed in that class. They eventually battled the public schools in trying to find appropriate services. His sister helped a bit, but his parents were the main source of support. "She was just along on the bandwagon."

The experience of attending a specialized school played a pivotal role in the positive development of his self-esteem. The

message at this high school was that he was as good as any
normal kid. He called his high school a "true support system."

S4 is aware that learning disabilities continue to affect him
emotionally in adult life. He sometimes is unsure if he should
disclose his learning disabilities to others. "I try not to let it
bother me, and sometimes I pretend not to let it bother me. It's
hard to tell somebody for the first time because of the way I
had been accepted before." He is "scared that they might call
me retarded." S4 has not erased the memories of being placed
in a class for students with mental retardation.

Much of S4's present social life is focused on his relationship
with his fiancée. His disclosure of learning disabilities was a
significant point in their relationship. He was a little nervous
and unsure when he first met her. "She's so incredibly smart,"
he stated, and added that she has a full scholarship and is going
to medical school. With typical humor laced with an underlying
fear, he related:

> I didn't want to spoil it by telling her (about LD). I didn't
> come out on the first date and tell her something 'cause I
> figured I'd date her and see if this is going to work out. Once
> I'd seen that it looked like we were going to be dating for
> awhile, I thought I'd tell her. So I told her. And that was
> hard, that I do have a problem. I told her about how it was,
> and she was curious about how it happened. She vaguely
> knew of learning disabilities, and she wanted to know basi-
> cally more about the other people in my school. Like, what
> were the emotional cases like? Or the dyslexic cases like?

S4 does not believe that his fiancée suspected that he had
learning disabilities before he told her. "There was just no way
that it ever could have come anywhere in the relationship unless
I went out of my way to put it in there." He summarized the
effect of his learning disabilities on her at the present time. "It
doesn't affect her. She's not embarrassed by it or anything. She
sees I'm not embarrassed by it. It's as if I was born without a
finger or something."

One of the positive experiences of S4's adult life has been a greater acceptance of his learning disabilities now as compared to during his childhood. "The older I get, the more readily people accept that I have a problem. When you get older and people get to know you without knowing your problem, and then they find out about the problem. They're more and more enlightened. They know more about it (and) become less negative. Turns actually from negative to curiosity."

As much as S4 seems to have achieved overall emotional and social satisfaction, areas of his life connected with learning disabilities do cause him anxiety. He presently lives at home and is worried about having the independent living skills to make it in his own apartment. He said he was anxious about keeping it clean, paying bills, and proving to himself that he can live away from his parents. At the same time, he expressed confidence that he would make the transition and felt it was important to do it before he gets married.

From the beginning of the interview, S4 clearly gave the impression of being sure of himself. He confirmed this impression when he said that he was proud of himself as an adult. "I mean, I've really come along fast. Some of the things I've done, places I've gotten to, I'm really proud of myself." He's proud because he's "had to hurdle some serious obstacles." In many ways, the challenge of overcoming the obstacles presented by learning disabilities has helped him grow as a person. His own self-esteem has profited from his success in coping with learning disabilities. "It's made me stronger," he said, "If I had to do it all over again, with the possibility of being learning disabled again, I think I'd pick LD. It's helped me. I mean it has held me back. It has made me stronger."[1]

---

1. S4 has reached a state at which future plans and dreams play a significant role. He has contemplated what will happen if his children have learning disabilities. He said that he would be vigilant to find an appropriate education for them. Other projections into the future are concerned with being comfortable. He thinks about having a "nice car, nice house," but he doesn't have aspirations to be extraordinarily wealthy. He is a little uncomfortable with his fiancée going to medical school in the fall. He ended the interview by affirming how willing he was to help other adults with learning disabilities and how enthusiastic he was about the investigators' project.

S5

It was hard to imagine that this outgoing young woman had once been a shy, quiet, and withdrawn child, but both S5 and her mother affirmed that before she went to high school, she was "a totally different person." S5 said, "you see these little kids that cling to their mothers' skirts. Well, that's how I used to be." Her mother added that "she was there, but she wasn't there." She was so quiet that she was a "perfect child, except for homework."

Homework was a problem because school was a problem. School was frustrating, especially because S5 felt that she didn't receive the individual attention from teachers that she needed. The early years of school might have been less negative "if they would have had more time to spend with each individual student. But they didn't. There were thirty kids in a class. How do you pick out one? And you could sit there for two hours and study your head off and still flunk. That happened a lot!"

The constant frustration and failure in school prevented her from building a sense of self-confidence: "I didn't have any." She responded to the painful experiences by finding ways to avoid the demands of school. "I'd get sick for tests." She didn't think that her teachers picked on her or made her feel dumb. The other students weren't as obliging. They teased her because she had so much difficulty keeping up with the rest of the class. She said, "They could be very cruel, and they were."

The teasing and concomitant frustration invariably led to lower self-esteem and greater insecurity. She didn't have a wide circle of friends. "I had three friends, and I was very protective of them." S5 believed her attitude stemmed from fear. She was afraid she'd lose her friends to someone else. She spent much of her time with her family. She was not really alone as a child, but she certainly had a sense of being isolated, of not quite fitting in with her peers at school.

S5 was emphatic that her life changed dramatically for the better when she started attending a private high school for students with learning disabilities. She referred to the significance of this event several times during the interview. At the beginning of the interview, she recounted, "I used to be very shy. I was so shy until I went to (the specialized school) really." On her first attempt to explain why the specialized school was such a powerfully positive experience, she laughingly postulated that the difference was "boys!" She had transferred from an all-girls high school. At the specialized school, with 110 boys but only 11 girls, S5 soon found herself to be the center of much attention.

Later in the interview, S5 ventured more reflections on her transformation at the specialized school. She developed much more confidence in this specialized educational environment than in any previous school setting. She described this growth as "the shell opening." She was able to point to a number of specific features of the clinical school that promoted the building of a stronger self-concept. "Having smaller class. Getting the teacher's attention more to you than the whole class. Like reading class—there was only three people in reading class." The teachers themselves were different than the ones from her past schools. They were encouraging and showed her ways to succeed at school. It seemed that the small class size, the emphasis on personal attention, the social opportunities, and a system that emphasized her strengths all contributed to her positive experience.

Not everyone reacted to this blossoming in a completely positive manner. S5 believed that her mother became overly restrictive. She wouldn't let S5 drive the family car even though she had taken driver's education and had received her license. "She (mother) told my sister that (the specialized school) really made me wild, and she was scared if I drove her car."

Nevertheless, life after the specialized school did not become reckless. S5 took her new-found self-confidence and made a relatively smooth transition from school to competitive employment. She had a number of successful employment experiences in which she was able to cope with having learning disabilities.

Because she had attended the specialized school, her learning disabilities were usually a matter of record when she applied for a training position or a job. She wasn't worried about revealing her learning disabilities to other employees since her job would not be jeopardized. In fact, she felt that she needed to reveal her learning difficulties in order not to create a misleading impression. Explaining her problems was particularly important when she worked under a supervisor at the local newspaper. "I was shy about it, but I feel she had to know because if I would have done it wrong, she would say, 'Girl, you're stupid!' And I'm not stupid. I'm just slow. I was called that a lot in high school."

She is willing to let some social acquaintances know that she has learning disabilities, but she chooses her confidants carefully. "It depends on the person. If it's somebody who's uppity, I don't say anything. But if it's somebody like J. (her best friend), I feel comfortable, and it's easy to talk a lot."

S5 gave a number of examples of how comfortable she is about her learning disabilities when she spends time with friends such as J. "I play scrabble with J. all the time. I say, 'Now tell me if this is right.' And I say out the word and she goes, 'No, it's backwards but it's right.' Or I'd come up with a word and I'd spell it. She goes, 'That's not a word, S5.' I'd say, 'It looks right in my brain!' But they know."

S5 stated that learning disabilities figure into her life in the specific ways she described but added that she copes "just fine." She does worry about tasks that demand reading and writing. She voiced concern about being able to help her son with school work when he gets older. At the present time, she tries to read to him, but he's too young to know the difference if she "messes up."

In most ways, her social life seems quite satisfactory. Her weeks are varied. She spends time with relatives. She bowls at least once per week. She goes to parties with her husband and is involved in a number of social activities that revolve around Mardi Gras. She has female friends in the neighborhood and one good friend from high school. She visits her friends in the neighborhood, and they visit her. She especially enjoys going shopping with her friends, particularly to garage sales.

In fact, when we asked her when she feels most comfortable and confident, she initially replied, "When I'm shopping." However, with a little more thought, she recounted an experience that seems connected to the obstacles she has faced because of learning disabilities. She feels really good about herself "when I finish reading a book." She added that when she did book-keeping at work, she took great pride "when I used to get the books to balance the first time. You sit there for an hour and it's still not balanced, and the boss is going 'I'm waiting.' But when you get it the first time, that's big. I feel that way when I do my checkbook, if it balances the first time."

S5 seems to have strong organizational and quantitative abilities. "I do all the bills. He (husband) don't even go get the check. I pick it up. He never sees it. I do all the house stuff." She is very proud of these skills, and with her mother present, she said, "I feel I'm more organized than my mother. She throws hers (family finances) in the desk and does them once a month. I do them every week." But with her characteristic self-deprecating humor she added that she's not particularly organized about housework. She doesn't get around to cleaning until evening and always has a sink full of dishes during the day.

S5 attributes her abilities to cope so well socially to her outgoing personality and her sense of humor. "If I was shy and scared to talk, it would be terrible." Being "bubbly" helps her get along. She described her own personality as "outgoing" and said, "I'm starved for attention. I'm always doing silly things . . . I think I'm outgoing. I do silly things, and I don't care what people think." S5 told us several times that she can easily laugh at herself, and this includes occasions when she makes "slipups" that seem related to learning disabilities. She summed up how learning disabilities affect her sense of self: "It doesn't hold me back. If it was to hold me back, I wouldn't be trying to go back to school." She knows what she wants in life, and she is aware of her strengths as well as her limitations. She has figured out how to cope.

S6

S6 sees himself as stubborn, as willing to face and overcome any challenge thrown his way. He's very clear as to why his personality developed in this manner. "My disability is one of the things that set me to be stubborn. When I was born, I was told I wasn't going to live." His mother, who apparently has a good measure of determination herself, simply refused to accept the prognosis. S6 paraphrased his mother's reaction to his birth. "'If God wants to take him away, let Him take him away. And there's nothing I can do about it. But give him a chance.' And that's where it all started. 'Cause I was told back when I was in grammar school, 'No, you can't do this. You won't amount to this. You won't be able to graduate from high school.'"

Apparently, telling S6 that he can't do something simply makes him determined to do it. "I've figured out in my life that there is so many people that are told 'no,' and they accept 'no' as the answer. If I set my mind to something, most of the time I do it one way or the other. I'm not easy to knock down."

Much of S6's life is a testament to his refusal to be knocked down. Getting through school was a problem, but he persisted. "When I graduated from high school in Boston, I wasn't on the honor roll, but I wasn't far behind. I graduated with a B average." Graduating from school was a significant accomplishment for S6, but it wasn't without a cost. "After graduating in '79, that was enough. That was a long and hard enough struggle to get to that point. And that was a goal that I had set that I was going to at least get that far." S6 is satisfied with having met that goal. He pointed out that although college is good for some people, many successful people have only finished high school.

His mother, who eventually became the president of the local Association for Children and Adults with Learning Disabilities (ACLD),[2] was especially sensitive to his learning problems. She sought out special schools and teachers and acted as an advocate for her son. At the same time, she didn't coddle him; she pushed him to succeed to the best of his abilities. "If it wouldn't have been for my mom, no matter how much my difficulties are, I wouldn't be where I am now." His mother has not stopped pushing him as an adult. She often reminds him to look for direction in his life.

As an adult, S6 is satisfied with his social and personal life. He largely supports his girlfriend and her children. He volunteers time to the Red Cross. He likes children (he worked in a camp in Maine for five years) and animals (he once had a job in a pet store). "I've had such a wide variety in a lot of things."

---

2. In 1989, the ACLD became the Learning Disabilities Association of America (LDA).

Leisure time activities include building up his stereo system. He is especially proud of his truck, a bright red, four-wheel-drive Chevrolet, and keeps it in immaculate condition. He has friends and enjoys going out with them. "I've always had a reasonably good social life because I was the one that wasn't afraid to go anyplace. I figured my friends would accept me for me."

S6 is proud of his ability to be independent through being a responsible employee. He does not seem to feel that he is held back by learning disabilities, even though many people would assume that his learning problems would prevent him from doing many things. He approaches his learning disabilities with a broad-minded philosophy. He doesn't really see himself as different from other people. His definition of learning disabilities (reported earlier) also depicts how he sees himself: "Everybody has a learning disability in one way or another. Everybody tries to put LD in a box. That can't be done. You have to poke some holes in the box and let some of it spread around."

Social/Emotional Summary for Subgroup 2

A common theme does seem to run through Subgroup 2. All members of this subgroup are happy individuals who have used either a sense of humor or a positive attitude (or both) to cope with the social and emotional demands of adult life. This almost cheery quality distinguishes these young adults from the other subgroups. In the case of each individual, a positive educational experience in a specialized school played a critical role in the development of successful social and emotional adaptation.

The importance of a beneficial secondary education becomes even more pronounced when early educational experiences are considered. For each of these young adults, the early years of school were fraught with frustration, embarrassment, pain, and difficulties with self-concept. Specialized education was helpful at least partially because of an inherent will or determination that these young adults possessed even at a young age. Even through the difficult years, they refused to be defeated. When they found an environment that responded to their needs, this source of strength fostered a bright, optimistic perspective. The members of Subgroup 2 are acutely aware that they have faced obstacles and overcome them. As a result, they all indicate that they are proud of themselves and their achievements. As S4 stated, "I've really come along fast.... I'm really proud of myself."

Life is not totally rosy. S4 and S5 have disclosed their learning disabilities to others, but they remain cautious about exposing themselves too quickly or to the wrong person. S4 and S5 expressed some worries about the future, especially regarding the ability to function independently. Conversely, S6 seems self-assured about his independence (although he tacitly admitted that his mother still plays a major role in determining future directions). In spite of an anxiety about the future, these adults with learning disabilities clearly leave the impression that they will be all right.

Subgroup 3

S7

S7 didn't tell us very much about his social life as he grew up, but he didn't hesitate to paint a clear picture of his social life in adulthood. "At the present time, my social life is kind of bleak," he stated. Even though S7 lives with his mother in a comfortable and well-appointed house in an affluent suburb, few aspects of his life seem to afford him the social satisfaction he desires. He reasons that everybody else is working when he has free time (he had experienced sustained unemployment) or that he's doing something when others have time. As S7 spoke, he began to offer more fundamental and reasonable explanations for the poor status of his social relationships.

Throughout the conversation, S7 indicated that he is frustrated by the lack of a close, personal relationship with a woman. He alluded to this concern several times, occasionally when it didn't seem directly related to a question. He said that his social life largely revolves around church activities such as a Bible study group, but it is "nothing like a date." A few moments later, he mentioned that he had "nothing like a romance right now." He declared that he was looking for a girlfriend, someone with similar moral standards, but that he was not necessarily inter-

ested in females from his church associations. Moreover, he feels
that he really does not have any close friends.

S7 disclosed that he does not make friends easily because he
is basically a shy person who is afraid of rejection. He worries
that he might "come on too strong or not strong enough." The
initial social interation is not a problem. He feels he is friendly
and is comfortable shaking hands on first meeting. But after an
exchange of greetings, S7 is often apprehensive about being able
to maintain his end of a conversation. He said that he sometimes
fails to understand conversations fully. As a result, he senses he
is prevented, in a way, from being close to others.

S7's life is not devoid of social activities. It is a priority for
him to keep "an open social life" with his relatives and immediate family. He summed up family activities by saying, "We
mainly eat together." He was not very explicit on what occasions
he spends time with relatives. He did explain that his relatives
are not around as much as he would like. He further mentioned
that he wishes he could be closer to his nieces and nephews as
they grow up.

The other major element of his social life is the church and
church-related activities. He attends Bible study regularly, which
gives him an opportunity for "conversations" with others. He
has participated on a number of mission teams. He pointed out
that it was "not just work all the time." Involvement with the
church also affords him chances to participate in such activities
as bowling outings. He is comfortable to an extent with the
people from his church, but feels that "their intellect is...higher
than mine.... I'm not as quick with words." Even in church
activities, S7 perceives himself as "separated" from others. He
doesn't spend much time thinking about whether he is as close
to others as he'd like. His relationships with members of his
church "come and go."

The spiritual qualities of church involvement are at least
equally important. He declared that he "couldn't do anything
without faith in Christ." His faith is "the only reason" he can
make it. Having disabilities has brought him closer to "the
Word." He believes that God guides him and feels that he is
strongest when he is in touch with God. "When I'm in myself,
I give up. When I find the Lord's will, I accomplish a lot...."

I get depressed sometimes when I'm away from the Lord." In spite of low moments, he sometimes experiences a kind of spiritual high where he feels that he's "on top of the world" and that he can "conquer." He also copes with daily stress through his faith. He is able to relax after he's prayed about a problem and prays more when he's under stress. He explained that prayer was effective for coping with emotional difficulties because the Lord "takes all the guilt." Consequently, the effect is "like a load off my mind." In terms of "his relationship with the Lord," the people at church do understand him.

S7 indicated that several sources of concern cause him anxiety. He worries that his mother will eventually die and that he will be on his own. He doubts that he will be able to make as successful a living as his father, a "workaholic" and "good at what he did." Unlike his father, who was a pioneering petroleum engineer and executive, "my abilities are limited to physical labor, nothing mental." Aware of his lack of money-making skills, S7 questions whether he can maintain the house, contribute to the world, and support a family. S7 was very clear that he would like to have his own family.

S7 readily acknowledges that he has a disability. One of the main effects of his self-esteem is that he believes he is realistic and accepting of his weak and strong points. When we asked him to describe himself, he enumerated both strengths and weaknesses. "Stressful, . . . aggravated, angry. . . . When I'm feeling good about myself, I feel successful. I feel good about myself because I'm able to overcome my handicaps." He derives a sense of accomplishment from completing tasks such as yard work because "it looks good." He tends to stay away from tasks such as woodworking because he gets "depressed" from the "figuring." S7 sees himself as lacking the perseverance for tasks that require much mental work.

S7 feels that having a disability and being aware of it have made him less successful and persistent than he would like to be. "I see other people with my problem and history. They have such success out of what course they took. They probably didn't know they had it. . . . They were forced to make do with what they had and not feel that because I know I have dyslexia, I guess I sort of make excuses for myself. . . . I can't do that because I'm too slow." Making excuses conflicts with the image the S7 wants to project for himself and others. "I don't like to say I'm a quitter."

In spite of difficulties imposed by his disability, S7 does have goals and dreams of being successful. He would like to "go out and play drums in a band and be successful." He sees himself as a nice person. He indicated that he certainly has sources of good feelings about himself, but learning disabilities make his life a constant struggle. "I think I've accomplished a lot, but there's a lot more I need to accomplish. (There's a) light at the end of the tunnel,... but someone's always adding an extension to the tunnel."

S8

S8 initially did not seem to feel that learning disabilities affected her family relationships. Reflecting on her past a little more, she tried to recollect the feelings that her memories evoked. Soon, she became aware that learning disabilities had colored many of her family experiences—perhaps to a degree that she wanted to forget. She said that whereas her parents didn't discuss her learning problem explicitly, "they knew I had a problem so they treated me a little differently than my sister and brother." In the early part of the interview, S8 remarked that "none of them put me down or anything like that," but upon reflection about her relationships with her siblings, she recalled some painful memories.

S8's older sister and younger brother didn't seem to understand her learning disabilities. They appeared to think that her difficulties at school resulted from a lack of intelligence. "Sometimes they would call me retarded or things like that. They would only call me that if they were mad at me. If I had done something wrong that made them mad, that's when they'd call me that." S8 talked about how it felt to be teased and labeled. Her siblings' taunts "didn't make me feel good. It made me think, 'Maybe I am ... (retarded), 'cause I'm in a different school.'"

When asked if she really believed she was retarded, she replied: "I'd look at myself. I'd look at myself in the mirror, and I'd say, 'Well, I guess I don't look that' (i.e., retarded). And then I'd question and ask my mom, and she'd say, 'No, no, you're just slow in learning.'" Throughout the difficult time growing up, she felt that her parents were supportive.

Indications of S8's learning problems appeared when she first attended school. She repeated first grade because of problems in spelling, math, and reading. At the end of the third grade in a regular parochial school, she entered a small, private clinical school for children with reading and learning difficulties. S8 stated that she profited from the specialized instruction, but she added, "I was separated. . . . I don't know if it was good that I was separated at (the specialized school)." S8 clearly had felt uncomfortable about not being in the mainstream. As she looked back over her time at the specialized school, she remembered that she wished simply to be like everybody else.

S8 questioned the effectiveness of receiving a special instructional program. She said that the teachers in this school may have been "too understanding." S8 thought that maybe she needed more "pressure." Apparently, she perceived that, because expectations were lower at the specialized school, she had not been pushed to learn academically. Instead, she learned to "get over on the system" and not do much schoolwork. S8 also expressed misgivings about having taken prescribed Ritalin during her time at the clinical school. "Maybe they should have just worked with my mind more than just give me the pill." All in all, life at the special school had made her feel separated from other kids. She felt that because of the "narrow life" at this special school, she had trouble communicating with her peers after she moved on to a regular private high school.

S8's learning problems had not disappeared by the time she left the special school. Instead, she entered a regular high school because she wanted to leave the stigmatizing experience of attending a special school and reenter the mainstream. As far as she knew, the high school she entered did not have special programs; she was able to get in this regular program because "they accept anybody." There were some problems at the start: she was placed in seventh grade even though she was fourteen. In spite of suffering some hurt at being older than her classmates, she was glad to be in a different environment. She felt that she "fit in" socially. She dated, and her social life in general was more active than it had been previously. "I just soon forgot about all the worries I had."

Did she stop feeling that she had learning disabilities? "I tried to keep it hidden. I hid it as best I could. And I didn't have that many friends, never had a lot of friends." In high school, she felt somewhat isolated because of differences she tried to hide, but even in the clinical school where her learning disabilities were openly acknowledged, friendships were hard to find. She felt the other children with learning disabilities at the clinic "weren't on my level." It was easier to "fit in" in high school because "nobody was really concentrating on me, 'cause everybody else was bad."

S8 continued to reflect on events of her past with what seemed to be a growing sense of sadness. She began to realize that the act of hiding her learning disabilities, of keeping a distance between a part of herself and those around her, might have disadvantaged her in making friends. She believed that the main effect had been "not being able to get closer—get along with them. I don't feel that I need them 'cause back then I didn't really have them."[3]

"I am happy as an adult," she continued. She described some of the social activities she enjoys with her husband. They have a fishing camp (cabin), and they often spend weekends restoring it. Numerous family activities include parties, weddings, and other social events such as trips to the New Orleans World's Fair. Family members visit them at their camp. S8 feels that her family life is "typical" and not affected by her learning dis-

---

3. The interviewer was becoming a little confused. As S8 was speaking, she had begun to look increasingly uncomfortable or even preoccupied with her memories. Suddenly, she began crying and left the room. Within a few minutes, she had composed herself and returned. Apparently, her own memories had caught her off guard, bringing back feelings she usually kept at a far distance. She apologized for not being stronger and added, "I don't know why it's getting me now . . . I don't know what's getting into me. I guess just bringing it back . . . I thought I had become a lot stronger, but I guess not . . . It was so painful back then." It would have been difficult if not unethical to push S8 further about the feelings she experienced while growing up.

abilities. She qualified this remark by saying, "I wouldn't say I'm the oddball of the family but just the more hyper one... the different one."

S8 took the time to give more thought about her social life as an adult. She felt that she didn't really have a circle of friends. She perhaps had more friends before she was married, but even then most of her social life revolved around her relationship with her future husband. When they first stared dating, "he didn't know anything about LD, and he'd say, 'Oh no, you just didn't study. You just clowned around—class clown.' So my mom kind of told him about it. I don't think he really understands the deep parts of it. But I think he will. But since I'm so far behind, maybe that's why I'm making the mistakes. But he never puts me down or anything like that. He helps."

Her mother continues to be a strong source of support, the one who understands best. After a bad day, S8 often calls her. S8 said that it's important to know she can talk to someone about the frustrations learning disabilities sometimes cause her. Her mother often tells her to "keep trying."

When S8 thought deeply about her past, she realized that learning disabilities had played a significant and painful role in her childhood. Now, as she described her present social life, she seemed to become increasingly aware of the influence of learning disabilities. For example, she admitted that some of the most stressful events in her everyday life involve going to the bank or grocery store where she has to write checks and make calculations. S8 still has great difficulty spelling words and performing basic arithmetic operations. She also feels anxiety if she has to "read something out loud to someone that doesn't understand" that she has a learning problem.

Interacting in social gatherings can also be a problem. She finds it difficult to talk in front of a group of people. "Sometimes I feel like I can, and sometimes I feel like I can't. If I felt comfortable with the people, I wouldn't mind." Nevertheless, she acknowledged that she sometimes has difficulty putting thoughts into words. "I might say something that's just a little bit off of what I'm supposed to be saying." She surmised that her anxiety was one of her emotional weaknesses but added that she was often "too hard" on herself.

Many aspects of S8's adult life are pleasant. She is aware that certain activities afford her satisfaction. "When I feel I've gotten something done, that's when I feel good. That's when I can relax. But if I'm just sitting around, it makes me nervous." Chores such as housework can be rewarding, especially if she has made a "good effort." The fact that she was making an effort to find a job was rewarding. "Even if I don't get one, at least I can say I tried. I like to try."

She considered herself outgoing, and she indeed was affable and personable throughout the interview. "I guess you could say I was a live one out of my side of the family." She stated that her greatest emotional strengths are her sense of humor and being "mentally strong." "I think I can handle some things more than others (i.e., other people)." Some of this mental toughness was a result of living with learning disabilities. It made her stronger. "I had to learn to accept it. I had to be open-minded, to realize that things are not all that bad." She feels that contending with learning disabilities has helped her develop in certain ways. "I feel that everybody should have some type of problem to make them realize that, to make them un-derstand other people's needs, to understand people better." S8 characterized herself as a caring person who envisioned herself as a social worker—but she didn't have the skills or background.

S8 showed that her social life had many facets. Learning disabilities do not enter into every aspect but still have a sig-nificant impact on her perceptions of herself. Most importantly, she spent and still seems to spend considerable energy trying to hide her learning disabilities. She clearly expressed discomfort over the sense of lying about something. For her, this deception was "maybe the worst pain."

S9

S9 was aware that learning disabilities had affected many areas of his life. He described how the socialization process was dif-ficult for him in school. The greatest difficulty for him was being "picked on." He said, "I was a regular punching bag." When asked why he thinks other kids picked on him, he blamed his father. "I think it was my dad's fault. He taught me to be nonviolent. And I just would love to kill him for it." He elaborated on his fate at school. "I wouldn't even defend myself. I'd just let them beat up on me. So I just learned to live with being a punching bag." S9 was not able to give other reasons for these childhood social problems. "I can't figure it out. Maybe jealousy. Most of the people that have picked on me usually were, like, scum bags. People with long hair and T-shirts and stuff." He added that the other boys may have picked on him "to get confidence in themselves, or they needed to beat up on somebody." He attempted to delineate some of the social-psychological variables, but was more focused on describing the physical bullying of "wedgies" and "redbellies."

S9 pinpointed a specific emotional experience in his school days that resulted from learning disabilities. Perceptual-motor coordination posed significant obstacles for him in school, especially with sports. He elaborated, "Like basketball, forget it! I could never deal with it. I couldn't walk and dribble at the same time. I'd have to seriously concentrate on it. To be able to move around people while they're coming down on you, it just seemed like I couldn't do it. I was on the basketball team, and I made a fool out of myself a lot of the time."

S9 said that he often did not know what to do with the ball when it was in his hands. "I'd be looking at all the other people on the team, and I wouldn't know who to throw it to. Then it'd be too late, and they'd knock the ball out of my hands. And I would be, just, lost. I'd sit on the bench more than I played." S9 described how the perceptual-motor difficulties with basketball made him feel. It was "a feeling of being boxed in or something. Everything is just closing in on me, and I can't deal with it. I'd just get rid of the ball. A lot of people were watching, like the whole gym is fixed on the ball, and you've got the ball. It's like, eyes staring at you or just looking at you."

The situations in which he felt overwhelmed (perhaps by sensory stimuli) caused emotional discomfort or anxiety. At times, this anxiety would exacerbate his inability to keep up with the other students. He said, "I would get all tensed up and get ready to do something, and then I wouldn't be able to do it. Then I'd be more or less just—not depressed—brought down. I can't do it. I'd just be bummed out."

S9 used the same metaphors to describe similar feelings and situations in adult life. When criticized for being slow (perhaps related to perceptual-motor difficulties), he gets a "'boxed-in feeling.' I feel like I'm two inches tall. I feel humiliated. Now I don't let it really ever bother me."

After facing a multitude of situations in which he was hampered by learning disabilities, S9 began to lose interest in school and became less motivated to learn. "I got to where I would say, 'I can't do it. I don't care about it. I don't need to learn how to do that.' And I would just not worry about learning it."

His experience at a clinical private high school, which had been so positive for some of the other interviewees, was not successful. His work was barely "C" level. He dropped out before his senior year. A recent visit to the school altered some of his perceptions about his education. "I went to (the specialized school) a couple of weeks ago, and there's chicks there now. Now they got girls, and it's like, yeah, I wanna go back. I missed the senior trip. That's one thing, and graduating."

S9 had a very simple description of the transition from school to adult life. He concluded that, "school's a really hectic place to go. You get beat up on the stuff. After you get out of school, it's kind of easy, but it's kind of tough as far as finances. That's the *only* thing you got to keep up."

Keeping up his finances has been difficult because he has had problems finding and keeping jobs. He provided us with some insights into how his social skills may diminish his employability. In one case, he tried to get a job he really wanted as a stereo installer. He spent much time on the application. He was upset when he was not offered the job immediately. He told them that he couldn't just sit around and wait to be called. Apparently, his prospective employer found S9's behavior bothersome and inappropriate. S9 left feeling frustrated and depressed, especially because he had convinced himself he'd be able to get the job.

His difficulties with work have created stress in his relationship with his mother. Perhaps because he doesn't live with his father, his father doesn't question him very much. His mother is convinced that he needs to do something and is very concerned about him. He said that she occasionally cries because he doesn't have a job. He admits that she is responsible for "putting a roof

over his head." "When I have a job," he said, "I give her the
money" in order to help out. He also explained that he has
other priorities for his money. He prefers to spend the money
on partying. "And that's really a waste of money. But it's nice.
Every time I go to spend fifty dollars, it's great—buy chicks
drinks—get on the good side of people—cool." It is not difficult
to imagine his mother's exasperation with his attitude about work
and money.

Since he stopped going to school, S9 has developed a small
circle of friends with whom he socializes regularly. Two of his
friends attended the specialized school with him. Another friend
"doesn't have any kind of a learning disability." A fourth friend
"has a small learning disability. But he just doesn't let it show.
It's not as bad as mine."

S9 has made a successful adaptation to adult life at one level
simply by having a circle of friends. But it is a circle whose
activities perhaps do not represent successful adult adaptation.
S9 described their typical social activities. "We just drive around,
get drunk. We drink every night practically. We don't go to bars
because they're too expensive. Sometimes we go to people's
houses. We like to go to the lake and sit out there, but the cops
always run us off. We spend our time running from place to
place. Every time we get kicked out we just jump in the car and
go somewhere else." In these descriptions of his social activity,
S9 demonstrates a kind of social vulnerability. He has seemingly
little social focus and is susceptible to behaving socially
inappropriately.

S9's circle of friends does provide some social benefits. He
is able to share the frustrations of having learning disabilities
with them. He feels that it's important to have friends who
understand him. "Yeah, all my good friends, I've told 'em,
'Look, I've got some problems. Let me try, and if I can't do
it. I'll tell you.'" If he can't do something, one of his friends
will help him. His friends look upon his shortcomings as natural
and normal. They treat him as a normal person. They take over
for him when there's too much pressure. S9 acknowledged that
having friends who understand his learning difficulties is very
important to him. He has been comfortable enough with this
group of friends to expose his difficulties. He added that the

activities that he and his friends undertake don't require "a lot of concentration." In this way, he attempts to structure his social life to minimize the interference of his learning disabilities.

Problems associated with learning disabilities do interfere with socializing with girls. He has problems talking to girls and is afraid that he'll stutter. He can make "small talk" but has trouble maintaining a real conversation. When he tries to think of other things to say, he "goes blank." Even before he begins to talk to a girl, he assumes that he'll make a bad impression. "I have a small vocabulary, and so whenever I use big words, sometimes I forget how to use them. And I'll say the wrong word. And sometimes I'll forget what I'm getting at, and then I'll forget which way I'm going. So the chicks will just sit there and look at me, and I will try and talk. I'd make sense, but I wouldn't be able to impress them. I'd just be able to make small talk, conversation. But that'll be a serious jam."

S9 has also experienced anxiety in social situations for reasons that are seemingly based in an adolescent subculture. He explained, "When I get real excited that the night's gonna go real good and something's gonna go right, I'll start getting all tense and happy. My heart'll start going real fast—two thousand times a minute. And pressure builds up—feels like a stabbing feeling every time my heart beats. Then I'll sit there a little while. Then I'll take some deep breaths and catch a head rush—pretty cool— maybe black out and get real light-headed. I mean it's not right, but it feels tripped out."

S9 indicated that he does have a girlfriend who has learning disabilities. She also attended the specialized school. He demonstrated an interesting mixture of compassion and insensitivity to her learning problems. He said that when she acts inappropriately, "I just let her get stupid." Because he doesn't want to embarrass her, "I'll just shut up. I try not to be better than her. I usually never try to outdo anybody."

Social/Emotional Summary for Subgroup 3

As might be expected, the members of Subgroup 3 are rated relatively low in their degree of social and emotional adaptation. S7 stated pointedly that his social life was "bleak." S8 clearly has a more active social life and has a marriage that fulfills many emotional needs that remain unmet in S7. However, she doesn't seem to have many friends, and her life revolves around her immediate family. S9 certainly is involved with a social circle, yet the satisfaction he finds in it is questionable; he seems to have many unfulfilled components socially and emotionally. All of these adults manifest a lack of real independence. S7 and S9 live with their mothers, and S8 is quite dependent on both her husband and immediate family.

All the members of Subgroup 3 acknowledged that learning disabilities sometimes interfere with their ability to communicate and to make the right impression. Perhaps for this reason, they tend to be more concerned about hiding their respective learning disabilities from others. Although S8 was able to see some pluses about having struggled with learning disabilities, as a group these individuals have not reaped the benefits that Subgroups 1 and 2 have experienced. Having learning disabilities has not produced a sense of determination or an indomitable will to succeed. Instead, the members of Subgroup 3 seem to be resigned to a life that has limited opportunities for social and emotional growth and satisfaction. Learning disabilities have resulted in a sense of separation from the social mainstream. Unfortunately for these adults, they do not appear to have a plan or a means to overcome this feeling of separation.

Social/Emotional Summary across all Subgroups

In reviewing the social and emotional domains across all subgroups, several themes culled from longitudinal and follow-up studies take on explicit and personal meaning. For all these individuals, their unique learning disabilities have persisted into adulthood with a direct effect on their social and emotional lives. The extent of the effect is at least partially related to severity. Subgroup 3, presumably the most severely disabled, has suffered the most severe repercussions. Subgroups 1 and 2 have fared much better. Nevertheless, all these adults have gone through painful experiences as a reuslt of struggling with learning disabilities.

Of particular interest is the overall successful adaptation of

Subgroup 2. Although rated lower than Subgroup 1 on a priori criteria, Subgroup 2 seems to have coped at least as successfully as Subgroup 1 in social and emotional adaptation. A unifying feature of Subgroup 2 was a successful and satisfying secondary school experience. Subgroup 1 members met the demands of secondary education, but with the exception of S1, it was not a particularly enjoyable or rewarding experience. Furthermore, even S1 was concerned that his high school experience was not conducive to social growth. In other words, the members of Subgroup 2 may have profited from more favorable social ecologies during the critical developmental period of adolescence. They are a testimonial to the importance of specialized programming for students with learning disabilities.

CHAPTER 6

Daily Living and Keys to Successful Adjustment

Subgroup 1

S1

Of all the adults with learning disabilities interviewed, S1 spoke the least about the effect of learning disabilities on his day-to-day life. His abilities to cope with the daily management and organization inherent to successful adult adaptation are presumably the most intact of the adults in the sample. This situation is not entirely surprising. S1's learning disabilities seem to be restricted to reading, and even in this area, his disability appears relatively mild. Consequently, the effect of learning disabilities on daily living may be more subtle and indirect. The impact of learning disabilities is, nevertheless, significant. S1 alluded to how learning disabilities may have forged adult personality traits that cause him to feel uncomfortable in a number of social situations. He also spoke throughout the interview about a strong sense of determination that has largely been a response to learning disabilities. This sense of determination pervades many aspects of his day-to-day life.

Determination is a key to S1's success, but it also has other consequences for daily living. He described some of the ways in which he has had to cope with the effect of such determination. It has made relaxation difficult for him. For many years, he pushed himself very hard and "was constantly anxious." He has begun to temper his drive. "The last four or five years, I believe, I'm beginning to learn how to relax and play a little more." He listed some of these activities as boating, sailing, fishing, and working around the house.

S1 clearly believed that he has been successful in spite of learning disabilities and to an extent because of them. His response to learning problems was an intense desire to overcome those difficulties. He explained that from an early age, "there was enough intelligence and just enough bullheaded determination that I was not going to be done in, and I was not going to be made a fool of, and I was not going to not do it, that I overcame some of the deficiencies in not being able to read . . . I had the determination to do it."

S1 attributed some of his drive and determination to an interaction of his upbringing and his native intelligence.

> I'm sure some of it was the old German-Teutonic hardheadedness of my father's background. I'm sure some of it was the moral strictures of my mother, who was so strict on moral principles. "You do what is right and avoid what is wrong." It was easy to translate from that mentality to "You bring home A's and B's." Why? Because it's the right thing to bring home A's and B's. Good boys work hard in school. Some of it was, I'm sure, my own intelligence. I'm smart enough to know that, being goal-oriented, if you want to get to the end of the tube, you've got to crawl through to the end of the tube. If it hurts your knees to crawl through the tube, it's tough. You've got to get to the other end.

Part of his desire to succeed arose from the hurt of being rejected, of being humiliated, of being set apart from his siblings and peers because he couldn't read. "From those negative vibrations grew the determination to excel. I did not want to be set apart. I was going to make it even if I had to put in more hours (than the other students). I was addicted to the idea of having to excel so that I wouldn't be set apart, so that I wouldn't be a failure, so that I wouldn't be made a fool out of."

S1 identified the fear of not succeeding in grammar school as a critical factor in his success. By high school, this fear was becoming transformed into an almost angry drive and determination. One teacher in particular drove him very hard in high school. "I developed so much of a hate for him that I was going to excel in spite of him." With retrospection, S1 acknowledged that this hate had turned into respect because he realized that the teacher had successfully motivated him. Buoyed by success forged through hard work and determination, S1 applied this formula in college and law school. "When I got into professional school, I was determined that I was going to graduate first in my class in law school. And I did. Why, I don't know."

S1 gave a thorough summary of all these experiences to explain his success. He began by referring to the "grace of God" and he continued:

> A will to win. A will to want to do it. Determination to excel. A background that said from way back then, "You can do it." The guidance that I got from my parents, from my maternal aunt, from my teachers at school. You can't underemphasize that at all. That's so important. Encouragement. Encouragement for these kids is ninety-five percent of the battle. And I'm sure whatever I've accomplished, as I look back on it, has been through the encouragement of my mentors, my parents, my tutors who kept saying and expecting you to accomplish. It becomes a way of life to accomplish. I guess that's the biggest step.
>
> I used to love to say, even though it sounds kind of trite, "I could walk through the walls, man." And if a person makes up his mind, if you sort of live your life with the idea that anything you want to do—go ahead, just do it . . . forget about the disabilities. If it takes you a little bit longer to get there, so what? You don't even think about it. You just go do it. (It's) sort of a blind quest.

This prescription for success dictated by S1 had numerous side effects. He mentioned that he needed some time before he was comfortable with his own desires. "A lot of years later, I think I've learned how to hone that determination. In middle years or probably even in college years, it was determination so rabid that sometimes I might even step on people in the way. It's only been in the late years that I've been able to hone that down and polish it a little bit. Sure, it's great to succeed. It's great to excel. It's fine to have determination. But you don't have to step on people." S1 has managed to succeed in spite of learning disabilities, but his accomplishments have exacted a sometimes painful toll.

As with many of the adults with learning disabilities we interviewed, S1 was able to offer a positive reaction to the impact of learning disabilities on his life. "You know, there's a plus side to it. Maybe if I didn't have difficulty with reading, maybe I wouldn't be so determined, and maybe I wouldn't have accomplished as much, or maybe I wouldn't have wanted to accomplish as much. There's a lot of good. There's a lot of plus that comes out."

S2

S2 did not feel that he has had to alter much of his day-to-day life because of learning disabilities. To an extent, the impact may be diminished in his mind because he simply does not take part in certain activities where learning disabilities would be problematic. He began the interview by stating that his learning disabilities don't really come up in social interactions except in terms of writing letters. His spelling is so poor that he simply does not attempt written correspondence.

S2's learning disabilities affect his day-to-day life in other specific circumstances. He has problems finding locations and has trouble giving or understanding directions. Because reading is a slow, laborious process, he doesn't like to read instructions and will assemble a product through his own logic. He is not insistent about taking this approach, but will try to follow directions if his wife reads them to him.

Although it is necessary to be organized in his professional life, S2's leisure time does not require structure. In fact, he enjoys unstructured days when he can leave something half finished. His leisure activities are purposely antithetical to his work. Because his work demands so much attention to scheduling, "If I have a day off, I'll try not to look at the clock," he explained.

For S2, a critical incident in his childhood helped him begin to cope with learning disabilities. Until second grade, S2 did not realize that his visual perception abilities were different from those of others. The world was a visually confusing place. Moreover, S2 had no frame of reference to sort out this confusion. One day in second grade, he suddenly realized that he saw things differently from the other kids. The classroom had a picture of a drum majorette in front of a band, but S2 could make no sense of it. Additionally, he didn't realize that other children could make sense of it. He recalled that later a significant development occurred:

> The most dramatic thing that ever happened to me was one day when I looked at a picture and couldn't perceive what the picture was about. That was significant. . . . I guess it was second grade. And every day I'd come in and wonder what that damn picture was in front of the class. And I'd look at it, and I'd look at it and have no idea what it was. It was just colors. It could have been modern art, just colors. They had no form, had no dimension. I could not begin to explain what it was. And then one day it clicked, and I was able to interpret what this picture was. And then I started to be able to interpret other paintings and photographs, some that I had grown up with around the house.

Having learning disabilities undoubtedly caused S2 to struggle with many facets of life. He felt that he has reaped some benefits from these struggles. "The only positive thing I see to it is that I feel like I work pretty hard at anything that I do. It's probably because I've had to work so hard to do a lot of these things, and maybe if it had come easier, I wouldn't have stuck to it." S2 stressed a number of times that learning disabilities had made him a more determined individual. He did not try to rationalize that he was fortunate to have learning disabilities. Instead, he tried to present a more balanced perspective about his disability.

Some of this balanced perspective emerged when he reflected on how the lives of some of his classmates from high school and college had progressed. Many of his friends were successful students who didn't have to work very hard. In some ways, they weren't as well prepared for adult life as S2. "I'm finding since graduation that you still have to work very hard in this life, and I think some of my friends have just quit too soon, before they achieved what they wanted to. . . . I just know that I have to work harder to accomplish." He said that he knew by the third grade that he'd have to work harder than others to be successful. His tenacity has given him a sense of confidence, for he knows

that if he has the necessary time to work at something, he will
be successful.

S2 repeated this theme of having learned to work hard a
number of times during the interview. When the interviewers
asked him why he was more successful than others, he responded
that he was the firstborn and was pushed hard by his parents.
In turn, he tried to fulfill their expectations of success. He had
to work especially hard in trying to please his parents. Apparently, the struggle was worthwhile for him. "It feels pretty good
to have accomplished some things," he said. He also indicated
that he might have become more successful than his two brothers
because their problems may have been greater than his own. "I
realize there are different levels of learning disabilities, and mine
may not be as severe."

Nevertheless, the overriding key to success for S2 has been
his tenacity. He doesn't think there are many reasons that he
has been able to accomplish a great deal. "Just one. Just perseverance. That's all. That's what I see."

Having learning disabilities has also afforded him an opportunity to be more empathetic. He feels he has a special ability
to understand his daughter, who has learning disabilities. He
can appreciate what she's going through academically because
he had a parallel experience. In at least one way, learning disabilities have made him a better father.

S3

S3 is conscious that she deals with learning disabilities in many
aspects of her daily life. She has integrated the effects of her
learning disabilities very adeptly. Consequently, she often doesn't
even consider that daily life could be different or easier if she
didn't have to deal with a disability. "I guess I've really come
to terms with some things. I never read a newspaper. I always
watch the news because why bother to read it." From her perspective, her lifestyle is adaptive and effective for meeting the
demands of daily living. She confidently expressed that "organ-
izationally, I've got it all together."

Her organizational skills are impressive, but her admitted lack
of flexibility often creates difficulties. She is comfortable with

her structures and routines but gets quite flustered if a routine is even slightly altered. She described a morning ritual where if she does any step or task out of the routine, "I'm lost. There are times when I'll lay back in bed and start all over again because I don't know where I left off. I can't remember where I am in the process."

It is essential that organization and routines remain constant. For example, she recounted that her kitchen is arranged in a specific fashion. Most implements are visible rather than put away because she would not be able to remember where to find them. Once, when her roommate changed the kitchen setup, S3 had great difficulty finding anything, and when she did, she couldn't remember where to return it. She had to reorganize the kitchen to her original plan. When she moved from her home state to the New Orleans area, she kept her kitchen set up in exactly the same way as previously. "I don't know if that's just because I'm stubborn or because it's comfortable."

The need for organization and structure seems to pervade her daily living. She mentioned that she imposes structure on everything from the arrangement of her medicine cabinet to her professional life. She has her work day carefully organized and keeps close track of all her appointments. She has trouble coping with unannounced appointments, meetings or activities. She said that if her work routine is interrupted in such a fashion, "I can't get it together."

Perceptual problems also affect day-to-day activities. "Sometimes I can't distinguish foreground and background. And there were a lot of times people thought I was antisocial. I'd just be sitting there, reading, (and) I can't distinguish between secretaries chatting (and) students asking for this and that. And a lot of times I get confused on who they're talking to. And I answer and they're not talking to me." She reiterated that if she knows what to expect, she is well prepared and does not become so easily confused.

Other discomforts indicate some auditory processing dysfunction. She considers herself very verbal and enjoys talking to individuals or groups. Talking on the telephone, however, presents difficulty. She said she can't always associate the sound of a word with the letters that make up that word. "When I was younger, I didn't verbalize letters. I didn't pronounce them all. So as a result, I just learned to watch people's lips." When she *sees* the letters being formed, she understands the word. When she cannot see the speaker's face, she has a hard time comprehending the sounds of the words. "The problem is that I don't have a hearing problem, but I've always compensated with the verbal skill of reading people's lips. I have a hard time verbally on the phone for a long period of time." She rated her greatest problems with communication as writing and talking on the phone and rated speaking in person as her forte. She consciously avoids using the phone and prefers to talk to friends in person.

Some perceptual difficulties reflect spatial disorientation and concomitant problems with following directions. "I can't remember sequences of streets. Many times I got lost, and I've learned that one of my releases is driving. I'll just go somewhere sometimes." Even though she would often lose her way, "I'd just go, and then eventually I'd be able to backtrack." Losing one's way would be frightening for many people. Instead, S3 has accepted her deficit with such creativity that she finds pleasure in not always knowing where she is.

In terms of her professional and social life, she cannot afford to get lost when trying to keep appointments in new places. To make sure that she'll be on time, she practices going to new places before she actually leaves. She practices both to reduce her anxiety about being on time as well as to conceptualize a visual road map. "So I'm going to go today to make sure I know where I'm going tomorrow." Her day-to-day life involves a great deal of preparation, "but I guess I don't view it as that because I've been doing it for years. That's just what I do."

As with the other successful adults with learning disabilities in this study, S3 owes much of her success to a sense of determination. At a relatively early age, she decided that she would take control of her life. She refused to be defeated by what others termed a handicap. She spoke repeatedly of her "inner drive." When she first learned that she had been diagnosed as having learning disabilities, it was very traumatic. Still, she resolved to move on with her life. "I did spend a lot of time (wondering) that I'm going to be this way if I don't make some changes, and I'm the only one that can." She did make changes and still does. The reader may remember that she resolved to start reading two years ago and has now read approximately four hundred books!

She learned to recognize her particular strengths and parlay them into success. Her verbal skills were obvious during the interview. These skills are an integral part of her professional and social life. She feels extremely confident with "anything that's related to verbal. It's very cut and dry for me. It's verbal skills I'm very comfortable with. That can be speaking in front of a group; that could be one-to-one."

S3 expressed satisfaction with her achievements as an adult. When she compares herself to her friends who also were tutored, she sees herself as having accomplished more in her professional life. "I feel like I have arrived in my own mind of what I thought as a child. I refuse to be a stupid dummy, and I don't think that I am. I think I've made it for myself."

Daily Living and Keys to Successful Adjustment
Summary for Subgroup 1

All the individuals in Subgroup 1 initially responded that learning disabilities do not play a prominent position in terms of day-to-day life. Upon greater reflection, they all detailed several aspects of daily living affected by learning disabilities. S3 seems to be the most involved in coping with the myriad manifestations of her learning disabilities. However, her learning disabilities are inherent to her lifestyle, and she simply doesn't appreciate that she has to put more preparation into daily living than others. Among other difficulties, S3 has problems with directions, a trait shared by S2. S1 and S2 enumerated the importance of relaxing, a skill that has often eluded S1.

This subgroup was extremely unified in identifying keys to success. These three adults with learning disabilities repeatedly cited determination and a will to succeed. All of them feel that they have developed strengths because of learning disabilities. They responded to their disabilities positively by working harder and longer than their peers. The motivation came from several sources. Partly from their own predispositions and upbringing, partly from fear, partly from the influence of significant others, and partly from a sense of truly believing in themselves, these individuals have all made successes of themselves.

A prescription for integrating a disability with success seems to issue from Subgroup 1: "Having things come easily doesn't always lead to success. Instead, success comes from having to struggle, having to face and overcome obstacles and handicaps." For these adults, strengths have evolved from weaknesses. All pointed to critical incidents that molded and intensified the will to succeed. The question remains as to how individuals with learning disabilities will find circumstances under which weaknesses can be transformed into strengths.

Subgroup 2

S4

S4 takes a realistic and pragmatic view about the impact of learning disabilities on his adult life. Having learning problems causes some inherent limitations. He feels that some young adults with learning disabilities waste time trying many different occupations instead of assessing strengths and weaknesses to find a single direction.

In spite of the boundaries that S4 perceives, he has made a successful adaptation to the demands of adult daily living. He likes to cook and cooks more than his girlfriend. He said he has no trouble making fancy dishes in terms of judging time or following directions. He rated his auditory memory as "OK."

His approach to organizing and sequencing may be influenced by his learning disabilities. When he worked as a waiter, he developed a special routine to keep his orders straight. He likes to systematize what he does and breaks down his work into sequenced tasks.

Problems with writing and spelling continue to interfere with daily living. "Yes, that slows me down." He said that writing a bill "gets in the way." He does some reading for pleasure and enjoys looking at newspapers and magazines. He doesn't usually read books. Learning problems do impose limitations, but S4's positive, confident, and realistic attitude minimizes those restrictions. For example, he has to do some reading at work and has sufficient skill to meet this requirement. He summed up much of his attitude about dealing with learning disabilities when he said that he's "not scared of reading."

S4 believes that a combination of factors has contributed to a feeling of satisfaction with himself and his life. Early moments of success laid a critical foundation. His talent in shooting made him aware that he was "as good at things as others. I think that brought me to the realization that it doesn't mean I'm retarded." When S4 freed himself from that label, he was able to make his best efforts to actualize his own goals.

Determination to succeed has played a large part in his success. He stated that he has the ability to work hard, "to work long hours and get up and go to school. And not only to do that but to achieve while going in both fields." His parents felt that he might have been pushing himself too hard, but that only made him more determined.

He has gained much confidence from the success he has attained in his work. School was difficult, but in adult life he has been less encumbered by learning disabilities. His success at work "let me know that there is something I can do. This is not what I really wanted to do, but I can go out, and I can look for other things. I can definitely achieve when I get out of school."

S4 has also found that certain aspects of his personality have been extremely useful in dealing with learning disabilities. He coped with failure at school through "my ability to divorce myself from certain situations. And what I would do was to divorce school from home. When I got home, school was at school. I worried about that then, but at home I was playing just like all the other normal kids. I do it to this day." He mentioned that he "divorced himself" from his mother having cancer when he was young.

S4's parents offered the kind of support that creates an environment where an individual has the greatest possibility of succeeding. In reflecting on the type of support and encouragement he has received from his parents, S4 offered these thoughts about interacting with individuals who are learning disabled:

I think the most important thing that I'd like to say is to try to treat somebody with an LD of any sort as if there's nothing special about them is the *wrong* way to do it. The ones who walk in with that attitude that you're not special, they're the wrong ones. We are special. We have disabilities. Just because our arms aren't crooked or our legs aren't crippled doesn't mean we're not disabled, 'cause we are. It's just the ones who do have their arms crippled and their legs crippled, they get special attention. People see that, and they feel sorry for them and think, "Oh well, they're special."

S5

S5's learning disabilities have had an impact on a number of aspects of day-to-day life. For her, difficulties with reading are a concern on a daily basis. Reading problems are so pronounced that she has trouble reading children's books to her young son. She manages to cope with this task largely because her son is too young to be aware of her difficulties. "I try to read books to my little boy, and I have to kind of make up words because I don't know the word." She is aware that this strategy will cease to be effective once her son is old enough to read himself. She questions how she'll be able to help her son with his schoolwork.

She is limited in the type of reading she does for her own interest. "I like to read books. But when it comes to contracts, Mom helps me out there." She has found an area of reading where her skills are sufficient; she feels she can understand all the material "perfectly" in Harlequin romances. Consequently, she truly enjoys reading these types of stories. When she reads other material that might be more complex, she employs a strategy similar to reading to her son. "I just kind of skip over. I don't skip over a lot, just the big ones (words). I kind of sound them out, and if it sounds right, I say 'OK' and I go on." She reads magazines for pleasure because the reading material is usually light, and the magazines have pictures. She doesn't read the daily paper, but did when she worked for the paper.

Much of her daily living revolves around housework and child-rearing. She is proud of her ability to manage the family finances.

She is satisfied with her housekeeping. Although she joked about having dirty dishes in the sink until after midnight, she does not consider herself to be a messy person.

She is presently considering going back to work and looks forward to the challenge of being a working mother. "When I go back to work, I'll have the house, the kids, and a job. And that's mind-boggling." It's "mind-boggling" to her because at one point in her life, she never imagined that she could be so competent. She said that she feels good about herself, knowing that she can handle the juggling act of job, house, and kids.

S5 delineated two distinct events that she feels helped her achieve a healthy self-concept and a sense of competence as an adult. She pointed out a number of times that her experience at the specialized school changed her from a shy, withdrawn, and insecure child to an outgoing, confident teenager and adult. She also indicated that her marriage also made a significantly positive impact on her development.

Her time at the specialized school helped her blossom socially. It also helped her take a more active role in her overall development. She said that the positive attention she received from teachers sensitive to learning disabilities stimulated "my eagerness to learn, my wanting to learn. I didn't want to do anything in the other school. I was just kind of there." At the specialized school, she became confident enough to want to learn and to achieve.

Her marriage represented an important step in becoming independent. Her parents did not want her to move out of the house while she was single. Marriage gave her a legitimate reason to assume a more adult role and decrease the dependence on her parents, which in many ways they fostered. Her status in her marriage makes her an equal partner and gives her adult responsibility. Her ability to cope with the demands of marriage and parenting has further increased her self-confidence.

S6

S6 credits many of his daily living skills to going away to school when he was a teenager. "I learned how to wash clothes and made my own bed, which I knew how to do before, but now it was something expected. I learned how to live in my dormitory with a bunch of odd people. A lot of kids can say, 'Hey, Mom, come do this,' and eventually mom will do it. But when you're in school like that, I thought it made me more mature. It made me grow up real fast." Life in boarding school necessitated independent living skills. He had to take care of himself, and he did. As a result, he feels confident about meeting the demands of independent adult living.

S6 exudes a sense of confidence that he can handle whatever arises. He related a recent incident in which his girlfriend's child was hit by a car. He immediately took care of the situation. "I had to be the one. She couldn't handle it. It was hard, but somebody had to do it." The willingness to confront difficult situations has been fostered by facing a number of difficult experiences in childhood. "I've been in situations. I lost my daddy when I was twelve years old. I was the one who found him. I was the one that called the ambulance. By the time my mom knew, everything was done." S6 reasons that being able to cope with such events in childhood has laid a foundation for confidence in daily living.

Reading problems associated with learning disabilities affect him in day-to-day life. "There's times when I read things that I still don't understand what they are. But if I go back and read it again and go back and read it again, I can figure it out." He gave an example of this problem when he was setting up his VCR. The directions were hard to comprehend. He read them a few times. When he had the basic idea, he asked his girlfriend to help. S6 does not seem embarrassed by reading difficulties. He does some reading for pleasure. He reads the newspaper "a lot" and peruses sports and leisure technology magazines.

Instead of feeling held back by the learning disabilities, he believes that he has overcome many of his learning problems. He does not reverse letters anymore. He has no trouble with fine motor skills, organization, figure-background, or concentration. "I find that I do a lot better than I used to do. I find that I'm a lot more calm in dealing with the situation."

The keys to S6's success in dealing effectively with many learning problems lie in positive educational experiences. The special instructional approach he received at the private residential school for learning disabilities unlocked the written world for him. "I remember calling my mama on the phone and telling my ma, 'Hey look, I've discovered that I can actually learn.' Because I was in an atmosphere where there was people that were trained to teach you. And if they had to bring you all the way back to the first letter of the alphabet or the first number of the number system fifty times, they would do it. If you had to go through a whole year of going from one to five or A to G, they would do it. If it took you ten years, they'd do it. But if you were making progress, and this is what it took, that's what they would do."

The realization that he could learn served as a foundation for building self-confidence. When he was attending the residential school, "I felt confident. They allowed me to feel confident. And I think a lot of the problems that occur these days are problems that they don't allow you to feel confident." Success does seem to breed success. S6 suggests that the important first step is giving the individual a chance to be successful.

Another key to success that S6 cited was having family support to overcome learning problems. In his case, his mother provided a force that propelled him toward successful adaptation. He said, "You've got to have a mother that pushes you and pushes you and says, 'You're gonna do it,' and 'I'm going to stand behind you as long as it takes to do it.'" His mother still encourages him today. "She pushes me ahead. She asks me what I'm going to do with my life. 'You know you've got to do something with your life. You can't depend upon this, and you can't depend upon that.' I'm the type of person, if I go someplace to apply for some position, I'll come back again. I'm going to find a way to get in there."

In common with most of the other adults with learning disabilities in this study, sheer determination has been a major factor for success in S6's life. From being knocked down so often, he learned to pull himself back up. He simply got fed up with being told that he wouldn't amount to much. Somehow, S6 knew that he could succeed. Telling him that he couldn't simply made him more determined.

Daily Living and Keys to Successful Adjustment
Summary for Subgroup 2

The individuals in Subgroup 2 share a sense of having successfully adapted to the demands of daily living as independent
adults. Each interview revealed a theme of independence. S6 sees
his strong sense of independence as one of his greatest strengths.
All the members of this group evidence high self-esteem in terms
of their abilities, what they can do and accomplish. Concurrently,
they do not allow their limitations to dominate their thoughts
or their actions. All reported continuing difficulties with various
components of written language, yet none see themselves as
defeated by these problems. S6 expressed that he thinks he's
actually corrected many of his learning problems.

These young adults perceive themselves as successful for several reasons. S4 and S6 explicity described themselves as determined, strong willed, and even stubborn. This tenacity was
largely a response to being told 'no' so often, but it also resulted
from other sources. S4 feels much of his determination is an
innate characteristic; S6 credited his mother as a driving force.
All the subjects identified critical incidents that have helped them
with successful adult adaptation. S5 feels her marriage has been
a prominent factor in her ability to feel autonomous. S4 and S5
stressed the importance of building on success. These three adults
once again credited their secondary school experience with making the critical difference. The perspectives offered by Subgroup
2 portend the necessity of providing appropriate, individualized
education as a means for realizing a satisfying adulthood.

Subgroup 3

S7

S7 expressed numerous concerns about the effect of learning
disabilities in day-to-day activities. He described a typical day.
He lives at home with his mother. He gets up and does housework
and tends the yard. Often he volunteers at his church. He quickly
alluded to the frustration of learning difficulties by adding that

he "sort of float(s) along. I get kind of concerned. My abilities really aren't good." S7 feels he knows how to do a lot of things but nothing of a skilled nature. One of his greatest difficulties is his inability to accomplish very much. Lack of motivation also is a problem. He'll slip into moods where he doesn't want to do anything. He tried to sum up his sense of daily life by saying, "I accomplish a lot, but not enough. Problem expressing myself, problems talking to people. (It's) kind of hard to have a conversation."

Difficulties with expressive language appear to plague S7 in many aspects of his daily life. Giving directions can be a difficult task for S7. He does not feel confident in his ability to instruct others through oral language. Instead, he often needs to draw directions or instructions on paper.

Problems with receptive language skills and directions also affect him in daily adult life. He said that he has trouble comprehending instructions and fears getting them wrong. S7 can't remember phone numbers or addresses. Reading road signs can pose significant obstacles. S7 recounted an incident in which he was trying to find Reserve, Louisiana. When he came to the sign, he read it as "Reverse" and became confused. Although he feels confident in his driving abilities, he has had some "fender benders." It is possible that these minor accidents may be related to the distractibility associated with learning disabilities.

Perhaps because of problems with directions and related difficulties, S7 often is not able to get to appointments on time. For example, if he only allows the time usually needed to make a trip, he will invariably arrive late. He compensates by making allowances and normally gives himself an extra half hour to get to an appointment. This strategy seems to work relatively well for him.

Certain aspects of his day-to-day life do afford him considerable pleasure. He termed himself an "amateur gourmet" who loves to cook. In this instance, learning disabilities do not interfere to an appreciable extent. He completed a McCall's cooking course and is able to follow recipes. He likes to buy "good food." It was obvious that he takes pride in his culinary skills. He also expressed a measure of self-respect stemming from his ability to manage money. He pointed out that he budgets and shops for food with his own money. Clearly, being competent at something he enjoys has increased his sense of autonomy.

S7's opportunities to travel have provided him fulfillment. Traveling has posed a challenge that he feels he has met successfully. He has been able to "go around the world in spite of (his) problems." He is proud of himself because he "had to make ways I could handle it." He used coping skills that had worked in other areas of his life.

He had learned some coping skills for traveling when he worked as a truck driver. He allowed ample time to get to places. He would look at maps and then mark out the route. Once he got used to taking a specific route, traveling was not a problem.

In spite of significant obstacles and setbacks in his adult life, S7 maintains a positive outlook by setting specific goals for himself. The most immediate concern involves learning to support himself independently so that he can eventually support a family. Even though it might seem reasonable that he would be preoccupied by his own difficulties, he explicitly desires to make a contribution to society. His religious convictions may have helped him to look beyond himself to be concerned with the needs of others. Perhaps the key to success for S7 is an empathy for others made meaningful through his own struggles.

S8

S8's problems with reading, spelling, and, to some extent, math continue to have an impact on her daily life. In some cases, she is able to cope simply by working hard at a task, but in other situations, she has had to devise some special coping mechanisms.

For example, her reading skills are adequate for specific situations not requiring high-level reading ability. She passed her driver's license exam without needing any special help on the written part, but she did need to study very hard for that part of the test. She can glean essential information from the newspaper. She is able to read and understand the classified ads when she is looking for work. For the most part, however, she doesn't really read the newspaper. She merely looks at it. In order for her to sit down and work through an article, "it really has to be something good so that way I wanna go back and reread it if I didn't understand something, 'cause I do have to go back." Motivation seems to be a key element in her willingness to undertake the struggle that reading often presents.

In other situations, problems resulting from learning disabilities become more acute. Banking is a particularly difficult feature of S8's daily living. For her, much of the difficulty lies with the mathematics involved in "dealing with the money. If I know I have to go to the bank, I'll get everything written out, and so I know what I have to do and what to say. But if I don't, if I have to get real quick to the bank and get some money, then that's when I get really nervous, and I try to avoid it."

S8 is very concerned that her difficulty in calculating will result in public embarrassment at the bank. This difficulty also causes her frustration in private. With much labor, she can balance the checkbook by using a calculator. Nevertheless, the process is so frustrating that she usually lets her father or husband balance the checkbook. "I don't do much of it 'cause I'm afraid, afraid of messing up, afraid of getting aggravated."

S8 tries to avoid frustrating herself by special coping mechanisms. She stressed the importance of preparing herself in advance for certain aspects of daily life. A perplexing experience that taxes S8's calculating and writing skills involves using either cash or personal checks at the grocery store. Consequently, she tries to plan ahead to avoid finding herself in an uncomfortable position. She explained that, "If I have cash and I have to spend, like say one hundred dollars, or if I have no other check—being able to figure in my head the amount of groceries that will come to one hundred dollars, that's when I really get nervous. I would rather bring a check and know that whatever the amount is, I can write it out, and I will be all right."

Even when she writes a check, she has to use special strategies to cope with spelling difficulties. She limits how much she buys because "I know that if I get a lot it's gonna be a lot, and I might not be able to spell if it's over a certain amount." She also has to use a special method to make sure she spells the name of the grocery store correctly. "When I know I'm going to the grocery store, I write down, say 'Canal Villere.' But the amount (is still difficult for her). One time I didn't know how to spell 'eight'—sometimes I know—so I just ask her because there was no one around. I think it was the 'e' and the 'i' that messed me up. A couple of times that's happened with three or thirty. I just wrote it wrong, and I just gave it to her. I prayed that she didn't say, 'This is wrong. Rewrite it.'" S8 clearly becomes uncomfortable in some everyday situations because of learning disabilities. She said that she hates to ask for help in public places because she's afraid that people will stare at her.

Problems with oral and written communication have also made some aspects of daily living difficult for S8. She cited several examples of trying to explain situations or to remember to give sufficient information to clerks or salespeople. She said, "At the bank one time I had written something wrong, and I had to explain it. I knew what I wanted, but I couldn't explain to her how I wrote that down." She also reflected that exchanging items at a clothing store could be problematic. "I just feel uncomfortable because I know that maybe I'm not going to be able to tell her (the salesperson) how much or the amount." In these and other situations, S8 clearly indicated that learning disabilities continue to present obstacles in day-to-day life. Moreover, she often feels embarrassed by her difficulties in dealing with commonplace events.

S8 does appear to cope more successfully with other aspects of adult life. She keeps track of what is needed for the kitchen. She is able to use cookbooks. Her house is kept immaculately and shows no signs of clutter or disorganization. Following directions for some recipes or for assembly can be troublesome occasionally, yet, she does not feel overwhelmed, perhaps because these are usually private activities. She pointed out that she is very punctual. She has a good sense of spatial direction but doesn't think she can use a road map. Instead, she learns to visualize a route. In fact, she gave us very clear directions to her house. She emphasized the important visual landmarks rather than relying on remembering 'left' and 'right.'

S8 sees herself as possessing a fighting spirit that does not give up easily. Much of her determination resulted from facing obstacles that arose from learning disabilities. "What makes me tick? What makes me so strong in wanting to succeed? I guess, as a child, always being pushed back." Her present goal is to earn a GED. She has been "pushed back" in her efforts to acquire a high school diploma in the past. Her strong will, forged through a childhood of frustration, makes her certain that she will eventually get her degree.

She might have accomplished other goals if she did not have learning disabilities. Nevertheless, she feels she has grown in ways that have made her a better person because of learning disabilities. "Sometimes I'm glad I have it, and sometimes I'm not. Maybe I'd have a college degree. Maybe I wouldn't have the common sense I have. That's why I'm glad I have it, and sometimes I'm, like, 'Why me? Why can't I be out there and have a career like all the other women are starting to have?' Maybe I wouldn't be as sensitive as I am if I didn't. Most of the time, I'm pretty glad I have it 'cause it's taught me a lot." S8 has tried to find a source of strength through adversity. Her ambivalence seems to be a natural adult adaptation to learning disabilities.

S9

S9 offered insights into many facets of daily life for a young adult with learning disabilities who struggles to cope with the adult world. He listed his interests as cars, stereos, carpentry, and landscaping. He added, "But I don't like to work." From what he told us, much of his day-to-day activities revolve around his car. He gave detailed reports about the histories of several of his cars. Although he did not directly relate learning disabilities to this aspect of his life, his own perceptions may reflect the impact of learning disabilities on much of his adult functioning.

Driving around is very important to S9. When his friends go somewhere, "I do all the driving. I can handle that." This ability might be a kind of key to success in that S9 feels good about his skills, but S9 seemed to focus on a maladaptive feature of his driving ability: "I drink and drive. I don't really care." He proceeded to explain that he can "smoke, drink, shift, and corner at the same time." This is the accomplishment of which he feels proud. He rationalizes that his approach is sensible because "I don't really need too much coordination now." He only needs it for emergencies. He said he knows what to do and has been able to avoid a lot of accidents.

S9 gave a lengthy account of his "pride and joy," a Camaro. He keeps it meticulously clean to a point where the steering wheel is slippery because it's been buffed so much. He recounted how he was able to buy a nice car even though he didn't have the money. "Well, that was a pretty good scheme. I told the bank that I worked with my uncle for two months. And I called him up and told him everything that I told the bank. And I wasn't really working with him. I didn't have a job. And I passed the loan, and I got a three thousand five hundred dollar loan. Mom put fourteen hundred dollars down." He spent two weeks looking for a more powerful car than a Camaro, but felt he found the best deal when he checked out a used Camaro. "And then the dude comes out and says three thousand eight hundred dollars. I was like, 'Whoa, I'll take it.' I didn't even test drive it or nothing. I wanted it."

S9's somewhat impulsive style may have had some repercussions. He immediately discovered that his car had mechanical problems. He first heard tapping and had a friend who was a mechanic work on it. He felt great because they finished and got the car together. He started the car and heard "a serious knock." His friend told him the engine had about a week before it would completely die. Instead of dealing with the engine problem, S9 simply drove off and shot a piston rod out the block and oil pan. He had to call a wrecker. It took a month and one thousand dollars to fix the car. "But still I guess it's a good deal."

He has spent considerable effort decorating his car and wanted to enter it in a show. "But I couldn't get all my stuff together." He also would like to replace the engine with a larger one. Speed is an important consideration. "It takes off pretty good from the start. But forget it, when it goes about 75 miles an hour, that's about the fastest it will go. I like to do 150 or 180. Great! I had a Thunderbird that did 150. That was all right." Where can he drive that fast? "On the interstate. We just dodge cars and stuff. It's pretty easy. You got to think, like, a mile ahead of yourself. I got the hang of that."

In spite of S9's professed ease at the wheel, problems associated with learning disabilities have periodically affected his driving. He has difficulties with directions. "I'll get twisted around, and it freaks me out." One wrong turn, even in a familiar area, can really disorient him. He has become lost on more than one occasion driving home from work. He believes he has overcome this problem. He is supposed to wear glasses when he drives but rarely does. As a result, he passes up street signs because he literally can't see them. In order to compensate, he memorizes landmarks. "I don't worry about street signs."

In addition to keeping up his car, S9 has other responsibilities such as taking care of his room. He generally tries to keep it clean although it occasionally becomes messy. He does maintenance work around his mother's house. He claimed, "If I moved out, the house would go to shambles." He also admitted, "Well, I killed the lawn. The front yard looks awful. One reason is me; one reason is my mom because she won't get the trees cut. Sun won't shine in." He takes better care of the backyard. "I keep that up great because it's in front of my house." He tends to the twenty-five dogs his mother breeds, sells, and shows. He hates taking daily care of the animals but complies because his mother is too busy. He doesn't like the responsibility of having to come home after work.

A pleasure that S9 has seemed to find in adult life is cooking. Even in this endeavor, his often "creative" approach frequently yields unsatisfactory results. "I like to make stuff that's weird. Like I made some oatmeal cookies, and I didn't have any oatmeal. I found this cereal that has oats and all kinds of grains and stuff. I just dumped it in there. It wasn't like cookies. It was more like runny stuff, like a cake or pie." He remedied the problem by adding flour and eggs. "It came out like cookies. I can eat them. Everybody else keeps taking little pieces and spitting them out." He acknowledged that people often do not like his dishes. Apparently, he doesn't always care for the taste of his own cooking. "I don't usually eat for taste anymore. I just eat it."

Overtly successful experiences seem to be rare for S9. But simply coping at all with the frustrations of learning disabilities in adulthood stands as a significant accomplishment. S9 does possess methods of dealing with life that give him a feeling of success. The car seems to be the major focus of his adult life. His car makes him feel good. "When I'm in my car, man, I feel like I'm great. I know it looks good. And when I'm away from my car, I feel like I've been ripped away from part of me."

He has discovered internal strengths and weaknesses and learned to capitalize on his strengths. For example, he found that he could learn to do a bike trick if he didn't think about it but just did it. "When I try things, they usually don't come out right, but when I just do it naturally, it comes out pretty good."

He takes pride in his car and driving. Maintaining his car has made him more aware that a key to success is the ability to make money. For some reason, that goal has been elusive. His frustration has perhaps led him to maintain a kind of longing for adolescence. "Well, when I was in school, my mother was a little richer, and I used to get a lot of money. Now I don't get that much money. Plus, Mom is like, 'Make your own money!' I used to have an excuse (i.e., school). Now I've got all the time in the world to make money so she says, 'Make it.'"

S9 feels that he could be more successful if he didn't have learning disabilities. What would life be like for him without learning disabilities? "I've thought of that. I've thought a lot of stuff like that. I would be able to do a lot of mental things."

Daily Living and Keys to Successful Adjustment
Summary for Subgroup 3

Subgroup 3 is relatively heterogeneous in adapting to the daily demands of adult life. S7 seems to have a melancholy aura; S8 is somewhat embarrassed; S9 appears to be a little oblivious to the effects of his learning disabilities. In spite of these differences, learning disabilities not only have an impact on daily living, but make adult life a constant source of struggle and frustration.

The adults in this group have recurrent difficulties with reading, writing, and social communication skills. S7 and S9 have significant difficulties with directions. The quality of S9's lifestyle is questionable.

The individuals in Subgroup 3 are less well adapted than the other subjects. Within this subgroup ranked as least adapted to adulthood, the effects of learning disabilities are more severe. These individuals' adaptations to situations can quickly fall apart if the learning disabilities are not carefully monitored. For example, if S8 does not prepare her banking carefully at home, she may be unable to complete the transaction at the bank.

The members of this group had less to say about success, probably because they have not had a plethora of successful experiences. All expressed a belief that they have been held back by learning disabilities. Only S8 could state that she has grown because of struggling with learning disabilities. For S7 and S9, the determination the other adults were able to cull from the struggle has not developed. The "gain from pain" formula has not been as effective for Subgroup 3.

Daily Living and Keys to Successful Adjustment
Summary across All Subgroups

As was the case with the social/emotional domain, Subgroup 2 rises above a priori ratings and shows successful adaptation to adult living. For the members of Subgroup 2, adulthood has given them the opportunity to escape from constant reminders of their limitations. By getting away from situations that demand reading or other problematic areas, they have found many strengths and abilities within themselves. Although the degree of adaptation is high for Subgroups 1 and 2, the persistence of learning disabilities is still evident. These adults are functioning successfully not because the learning disabilities have disappeared but because they have developed means to cope. For Subgroup 3, the higher degree of disability may have been more overpowering.

It is clear that the individuals who see themselves as successful credit learning disabilities with having helped them forge a will to succeed. Those with less satisfying lives feel held back by learning disabilities. Undoubtedly, an interaction of many complex and subtle variables is responsible for these interindividual differences.

CHAPTER 7

Conclusion

It is not surprising to discover that the profiles of adults in the learning disabled population are rather varied. A continuum of functioning exists in all areas of investigation for each of the study's subjects. As is shown in the monograph, some adults with learning disabilities are highly successful and some are marginally adjusted. The major themes outlined in the earlier chapter entitled "Review of the Literature"—severity, persistence of disability, and effect of social ecologies—provide a framework for understanding adjustment at the adult level of development. In most cases, the degree to which each subject with learning disabilities relates to these key variables is predictive of adjustment. At the same time, there are a number of notable surprises.

When one considers severity, it becomes obvious that those adults with the most severe learning disabilities are having the most difficult time in adulthood. This is not surprising, but their degree of dependency is of great concern, especially since most of the subjects are relatively young. The prospect of lifelong dependency is obvious. The most severely disabled adults hold no plans for the future and suffer from the struggles of the past. It would seem that the situation has little likelihood of improving and may deteriorate with the loss of parents or spouses who are currently providing support.

The subjects with the most severe learning disabilities are disabled because the effects of their disabilities are global. To a large extent, these individuals can draw from only limited resources. They become prisoners of their disability with few pathways to escape. They have no high school degree, and their academic skills are inadequate. There are problems in attention, comprehension, self-concept, self-esteem, and social skills. Problems of vocational planning persist, and direction regarding any specific training is absent. Perhaps one could say that their fate was predictable. But would they be in such a predicament if they had received a well-tailored educational program? The existing literature (e.g., Balow and Bloomquist 1965; Hardy 1968) suggests that such a program alone would not have changed the outcome appreciably. However, other research (Rogan and Hartman 1976; Abbott and Frank 1975; Rawson 1968) indicated that an appropriate educational program in the context of favorable social ecologies could alter this prognosis. It does seem that each of the marginally adjusted adults in this study possibly could have done better, however.

Residual learning disabilities in the moderately and highly adjusted groups seem to be a comparatively lesser issue. Yet, notable problems are described in each subject's history. In some cases, the problem was relatively specific (e.g., the attorney's reading problem and the electrician's spelling and writing problem). Subjects with more global problems were able to compensate for them or devise bypass strategies. Oftentimes, they compensated in ways that led to favorable outcomes. In the case of the middle group, highly developed social skills became a major asset.

One should be cautioned against dismissing the severity issue for the moderately and highly adjusted groups. The notion that learning disabilities is a mildly disabling condition should be vigorously rejected (at least in this sample). One should not confuse the degree of accomplishment with a lesser degree of severity. The data presented in this monograph bear this out. To a large extent, what has been accomplished in these two groups has come from determination to succeed against the odds. This has meant working harder than any other classmates just to stay current. Moreover, a high cost has been paid in order to go beyond merely staying at pace with the rest of the class.

Those in the top two categories entered adulthood being very well aware of their strengths and weaknesses. They have predicated their adult adjustment on knowing what they can accomplish and what they cannot. They have made intricate accommodations for themselves and have put compensatory systems into place at home and at work. One can easily gain an understanding of why they have done so well, but what can be easily overlooked is their daily struggle to perform. In many circumstances, they have found the path to facile adjustment, but in other instances they must grapple with a new situation (whether routine or complex) that can only be mastered by calling upon their best energies.

The persistence of learning disabilities into adulthood is a theme that underscores the experience of all subjects in this monograph. Persistence can be the most debilitating aspect of the adult experience. Most often, learning disabilities are not outgrown. Moreover, learning disabilities do not magically vanish after the school-age years. What has been clearly seen in this investigation is the persisting effects of learning disabilities in all domains of adult experiences. The effects are omnipresent in all the study's subgroups.

Academic retardation is of course a persisting issue. Certainly it is just one part of the constellation of persisting problems for the marginally adjusted group. A myriad of other problems in adulthood emanates from earlier levels of development. So too, persisting problems abound in the experiences of the subjects from the other groups as well. These permeate daily routines at work and in their personal lives. The ethnographic format provides many rich illustrative examples of persisting problems.

Social ecologies can be viewed from various perspectives. In the case of the subjects of this study, one can surmise that their families have been supportive during their formative years as well as during their adult years. Parents, largely educated and middle class, have sought out the best services they thought possible for their children. They were their children's advocates each step of the way and their cheerleaders for each developmental, academic, and social task. But it is quite obvious that an intact, supportive family situation does not automatically ensure successful adult functioning. Conversely, a rather dysfunctional family system probably would put adults at greater risk. This may be true of the marginally adjusted group in this study.

The ultimate outcomes of the study's subjects seem to be unpredictable in terms of the socioeconomic and educational status of the parents, variables that have been held relatively constant in this study. But these variables may play a role in conjunction with other variables. Surely, social ecological variables such as type of class placement and status and success within peer group are important as well.

As for differences in outcomes with respect to P.L. 94–142, little can be generalized from this study. The group of highly successful adults became successful without benefiting from the broad mandates of process and programming of the federal law. They moved through the educational system before there was a mandatory special education law. Most of the subjects in Subgroups 2 and 3 attended school before and after the passage of P.L. 94–142. Conclusions on the effectiveness of the law are limited because these subjects did not really feel the impact of mandated programs—especially after they entered privately run programs. To a large extent, then, the subjects in this study may be thought of as predominantly a pre–P.L. 94–142 group whose outcomes emanate from a wide array of educational services not uniformly set by law.

The reader of this monograph should gain an appreciation for the complexities of adulthood when learning disabilities are superimposed on it. Most importantly, one must understand that this problem may not be mitigated with age and may in fact continue to evolve within the various phases of adult development. The implications of learning disabilities for the entire lifespan still remain to be studied. All in all, this effort and others have contributed to the growing recognition that the years beyond schooling, which can account for up to seventy-five percent of one's life, need to be studied and understood.

Concluding Thoughts on Adults with Learning Disabilities

A strong theme, almost a plea, permeated our conversations with adults with learning disabilities: "We are not that different from you or anyone else." Sometimes this reminder was expressed in words; more often it was implied in the accounts of the experiences these adults have endured. Was the quality of those experiences affected by learning disabilites? The effect is ingrained in every page of the interview transcripts. They have suffered and struggled. Can we use their experiences to help them? In many ways, they've already profited from the "school of hard knocks." Perhaps it is they who can help us.

The title alone of this section seems presumptuous. It presupposes that we, the non-learning-disabled, are better equipped to understand adults with learning disabilities than they are themselves. How can we, standing on the outside, hand down our pronouncements about what makes them tick? They've already told us.

In traditional forms of educational research, "raw" data are not enough. Data become meaningful through mathematical manipulations and considered interpretation. The experiences these adults shared with us cannot be manipulated to provide meaning. And if we're searching for interpretation, the adults in these pages have given enormous thought and effort to a myriad of implications from their own life stories. That thought and effort are overpoweringly present in S1's concerted and on-going struggle to understand his inner self in relation to the impositions of learning disabilities. Certainly, all the members of Subgroups 1 and 2 took advantage of the interview process to introspect. Such insights may not be as readily forthcoming from Subgroup 3 until we remember specific gems that their visions of the world offered us. The reader might consider what levels of synthesis and analysis are proffered by S7's visually poetic metaphor of learning disabilities as a video camera that reverses images.

Rather than try to take the words out of their mouths by substituting our own, it seems inherently more sensible to respond to the meaning that is already present in their stories, individually and collectively. Ultimately, their stories demand a response. And much of that response is necessarily a private and intimate act demanding soul-searching of our own. The response is not so much how we look at adults with learning disabilities as how we look at ourselves.

The experiences of the adults with learning disabilities in this study may stand as a model to which our own experiences may be compared. To what extent do any of us have the persistence, determination, and indomitable will to succeed as related in the accounts of Subgroup 1? If the will to succeed is born of suffering, then we can and should become stronger in response to the trials and tribulations we inevitably face. Undoubtedly, many of us fall short in this type of character development. It certainly requires courage to turn losses to victories. Within Subgroup 1, we witness a testimony to exactly this strength of the human spirit. S1, S2, and S3 remind us that accomplishments are not so much a result of luck or even "natural" ability but of plain hard work and drive. Hence, the issue of success becomes largely a matter of choice: Hard work is an option open to anyone.

The members of Subgroup 2 leave a similar message with a special focus on maintaining a positive attitude. Recent psychological and medical research has begun to draw attention to the psychophysiological benefits of laughter and humor. The good-naturedness of S4, S5 and S6 was an unmistakable quality. To an extent, it has been a key to their survival. Again, their experiences can act as a standard against which we may measure our own. We should ask ourselves if or how we would maintain faith, optimism, and simply a sense of humor after attending eighteen different schools, including a stint in a class for the mentally retarded (S4); after being labeled mentally retarded by a grade school principal or being denied classes in vocational training (S5); or after contending with physical as well as learning disabilities (S6).

The adults with learning disabilities in Subgroup 3 also offer us a chance to introspect and grow. All of us can identify with feelings of fear, frustration, and failure. Simply to be able to offer empathy to those who struggle is a measure of growth. The experiences of S7, S8, and S9 can help us embrace humanity with a greater realization of our mutual similarities rather than differences. We share the same dreams, hopes, and aspirations, and when they are not met, we share the same pain.

We have been privileged to enter the inner world of nine complex individuals. They provided a passport allowing us to enter into the private sanctums of their lives. Such trust was based on the faith that we would report their stories with honesty and candor. They all believed that their experiences might be able to help others with and without learning disabilities.

This trust carries with it a responsibility and commitment. Their stories are now our stories. We must share their pain and happiness, for if their lives do not touch our own, then we have gained nothing. We try to understand others through ourselves, our own experiences; here, we have an opportunity to understand ourselves through others. The experiences shared by these nine adults may offer a reflection of our own struggles.

Collectively, they have shared an essential ingredient of the human condition that many of us find frightening to face—vulnerability. All of them have suffered largely because they were guilty of learning in different ways from the supposedly uniform way the rest of us learn. Yet, they were hardly incapable of learning.

The adults with learning disabilities in this study offer convincing evidence that learning disabilities do not prevent learning from taking place. To some extent, it was the educational system that played the major role in making learning difficult. S1, S2, and S3 all have advanced degrees. S4, S5, and S6 are all active, productive, and intelligent members of society. S7, S8, and S9 continue to struggle. They have fallen victim to an ecological interaction of variables that has made certain aspects of learning extremely frustrating. The tragedy is that the situation is alterable.

These adults with learning disabilities may make the most significant statement through what they give to a world that didn't give them much of a chance. S1, S2, and S3 make professional contributions every day. The obstacles to success presented by learning disabilities would deter many of us. Instead, they have found ways to accentuate their abilities and to compensate for their areas of weaknesss. S4, S5, and S6 bring warmth and humor and a positive message to all of us. We can gain perspective on our own personal happiness from listening to these survivors who refuse to buckle to a negative outlook. S7, S8, and S9 seem to swim eternally against the current. They persevere with hopes and dreams. If they fail, it is our tragedy as well as theirs. We cannot be complacent when individuals who do not measure up to anachronistic notions of human worth are set adrift. These individuals should remind us that the human experience can not be reduced to a single set of standards implied by the label learning disabilities.

Most of these adults feel stronger for having had to struggle. Much of what we take for granted has required monumental sacrifices. They've had to be strong simply to hang on. Their stories can provide inspiration for the rest of us.

CHAPTER 8

Epilogue

The goal of allowing adults with learning disabilities to speak for themselves necessitates an approach that by design places the data as the primary source of discovery and learning and allows in-depth analysis to play a secondary role. As has been seen in an intimate look at nine adults with learning disabilities, the permutations of experience are astronomical in number. Similarities and differences can be generalized but at the expense of losing the unique aspects of each individual's experience. Thus, often the authors' comments are kept brief even when opportunities for in-depth analysis presented themselves. Furthermore, because of the scope of the study, generalizing to the entire population of adults with learning disabilities should be viewed as inconclusive at this time.

Those who read this monograph should leave it with a notion that the data presented are on one level simplistic and on another level complex. The monograph is simplistic because it is a look at nine adults in a universe of thousands. Moreover, it raises scientific questions that traditionally emerge using small samples. Yet, the data become complex when a realization emerges: Any attempt to represent the life situations of adults with learning disabilities can only be accomplished when heterogeneity and intraindividual differences are truly acknowledged.

The authors present this work to the field with the hope that further investigations adopt this method of inquiry. The value of the interview format lies as much in the questions that are raised as in the answers that are provided. It is of utmost importance that the field proceed to develop a deeper and richer understanding of adults with learning disabilities. This initial effort, the authors believe, has shown the potential of what may be perceived as an alternative approach to research. After countless months of working on this project, the authors now fully appreciate the utility of the approach.

Appendixes

Interview Form

Interview Form

Name: _____ Date: _____

I. **Observation of Setting:**

Where?

When?

Other people present?

Overall impression of mood and/or atmosphere?

II. **Demographic Information:**

Age

Physical Characteristics

Atypical Physical Characteristics

Marital Status

Children

Homeowner/Renter

Income Bracket

Profession/Job

Professional Affiliations

College Degrees Attained

Interests and Hobbies

Statement: "As you know, the purpose of the study is to talk about and look at the ways you've successfully adapted to adult life. In order to understand the keys to your adjustment, it might be helpful to think of some of the ways learning disabilities have affected or continue to affect your life and what you did or are doing to cope with those situations.

"We're going to cover different aspects of adult life. Let's begin by talking about your social life."

I. **Social**

Tell me something about your social life.

Do you belong to any social groups or organizations, etc.?

What kinds of social activities do you participate in? How often, long, etc.?

Tell us about your friends.

Do you have many? Any close ones?

Do you make friends easily?

What do you think are your strong points for making friends? Weak points?

Do you communicate well with friends? Social acquaintances?

In what situations do you feel best about your communication skills? Worst?

How do you feel when you're in a large social gathering?

How would you feel if you had to talk to a large group?

Would you mind telling us about your family?

How would you describe your overall family relationships?

Are others in your family aware of your learning disabilities?

** How have your learning disabilities affected your social life, especially in those aspects that we've discussed? Are there any problems of which you are aware? Any advantages? Is there anything else you would like to add regarding your social life?

II. **Emotional**

Can you think of some adjectives or words that describe you emotionally?

When do you feel most anxious? Least anxious?

What do you think contributes most as stress or anxiety factors?

What do you think contributes most to good and relaxed
feelings about yourself?

How do you relieve stress?

Do you consider yourself introverted or extroverted? Why?

What are your most persistent emotional problems or weaknesses? Are there patterns?

What are your emotional strengths?

How would you describe your self-esteem?

** How have your learning disabilities affected your emotional development and present emotional functioning?
Problems and/or advantages? Is there anything else you
would like to add regarding your emotional life?

III. Vocational

What kinds of vocational preparation have you had?

What kinds of jobs did you have before this one?

Did you have any problems with any of these jobs?

What is your present vocational status?

How did you find your present job?

What about your job do you find satisfying? Not satisfying?

Do you have any particular problems with this job?
Strengths?

How would you assess your own job performance?

How do you get along with your fellow employees?

Do you feel more comfortable dealing with people you supervise or with people who supervise you? Why?

What kind of reading, writing, and math skills are necessary
for your job?

Do any of these areas pose difficulties for you? What do
you do about it?

In what ways were you most prepared for your job? Least?

Have there been any accommodations that you've had to
make or have been made for you?

What has surprised you most about your job?

** How have learning disabilities affected your vocational
experiences? Did they influence your choice of profession? If you had it to do over, would you choose the

same profession? Why? Is there anything else you would like to add about your work life?

IV. Educational

How has your educational experience affected you as an adult? Relevant? Useful?

How would you assess your academic skills (i.e., reading, math, writing)?

Describe your postsecondary preparation.

What was the most valuable in your education?

Did you receive any label when you were in school? What was it? How did it affect you?

Were you in a special education program? How long?

Did you receive support services?

Why did you leave school?

Have you received any support services since leaving school?

What, if any, do you feel are your present educational needs?

** How have learning disabilities affected your educational experience(s)? Do they continue to affect your ability to deal with tasks requiring reading, writing, or math? Is there anything else you would like to add about your educational experiences/needs?

V. Daily Living

Are you dependent on driving? Do you drive? Comments.

What is your living situation?

How is money managed in your life?

Do you cook? Do you ever have problems with instructions?

Do you have problems being on time? Finding places, etc.?

Are you aware of being dependent on others for some daily living activities? Are others dependent on you?

Could you please talk about leisure time and time management?

What are your views on parenting and/or being a parent?

** How have learning disabilities affected your daily living? Is there anything else you would like to add about your daily living experiences/needs?

VI. General Follow-up Questions

What has worked for you in adapting to adult life?

Where do problems still exist?

How do you define learning disabilities?

In your opinion, do learning disabilities persist for you? How?

What are your goals and/or predictions for your future?

What have been the keys to your success?

What could increase your success?

What has worked against your success?

Where do you think you would be today if you did not have a learning disability?

Interviews with S2 and S7

Interview with S2

Q. What I'd like to do is begin the interview with some trivial questions. How old are you?

A. Thirty-nine

Q. How many children do you have?

A. Three. Two girls and a boy.

Q. You are a practicing dentist, aren't you?

A. Yes. But I also am on faculty at L— Dental School.

Q. Where do you practice, and what do you practice?

A. I practice in a suburban area outside of New Orleans. Now I'm limited pretty much to geriatrics.

Q. As a practicing professional, what professional affiliations do you have, and what organizations do you currently belong to?

A. Well, outside the standard dental, do you want those, standard dental organizations?

Q. Yes, like L—.

A. L— Dental Association, N— Dental Association, A— Dental Association, and I'm on the board of the grandparents, foster grandparent program.

Q. Do you have any affiliations in academic dentistry or something like that?

A. No. Just an advisory group that works only on particular issues. The committee has met, but I haven't even been to the first meeting. I have some other appointments through the school. New Orleans Home Rehabilitation Quality Assurance, and I'm also consultant to other organizations which are outside the L— Dental School. And then I have a private practice. That keeps me busy.

Q. What academic degrees do you hold?

A. D.D.S. and M.Ed.

Q. M.Ed., is that in special education?

A. No. That was in curriculum development (curriculum and instruction).

Q. Outside of your professional life, what are your interests, your hobbies?

A. Oh, I enjoy gardening, camping, outdoor life, that sort of thing, getting out of the office. I enjoy fishing and dancing also.

Q. Do you and your wife go out?

A. Sometimes. Usually with C—— and E——, who are real good friends.

Q. The purpose of our study is to look at and talk about the ways in which you have succeeded in your adult life, and to understand what are your keys to success. In order to understand them, however, it might be helpful in a very general way to focus on some of the ways that learning disabilities have affected or continue to affect your life. Also, what you did or are doing to cope with your learning disabilities and how you have accepted them. I've divided up the flow of this interview into different aspects of adult life. It is generally straightforward the way the interview is laid out. I'd like to begin talking about your social life, basically in very general terms. Then, if you wish, we can get some more specifics. Again, coming back to your social life, generally, how do you think you would evaluate your social life?

A. I think I have a reasonably good social life, I mean, for a married man. We have a lot of friends. I don't know exactly how learning disabilities has affected my social life because it's pretty well hidden and my disabilities. I don't believe my problems would come up in social interactions, perhaps only in letter writing. Through inspection, people would find out immediately that my spelling is atrocious, reverse letters and that sort of thing. But other than that, I don't see how, I can't think of any way it would come to play.

Q. I'm going to also ask a lot of questions that try to get to positive aspects of your learning disability too. So, if you don't mind, I'll go ahead and ask you some questions.

A. Oh, certainly.

Q. Simply trying to get a picture of where you are as an adult. What kinds of social activities do you participate in?

A. Well, we, I guess, the biggest social activities revolve around the children now. The children on picnics and school functions, you know, PTA meetings. Trying to think of other social functions. Occasionally eating out with friends. We've been to, over the past year, to crawfish boils (feast) and dental school functions. Last Saturday, we had dinner with my sister and her husband. We missed a school barbecue a couple of weeks ago.

Q. Generally, do you see yourself, your social experiences as being different from what my experience would be?

A. No, we take in a show, bring the kids to the show, we'll have dinner with friends or have picnics with families. In general, I dated a lot before I got married. I dated very actively in high school and went to a lot of Mardi Gras balls.

Q. Is there any social experience that you'd shy away from in any way that would be any different from what I'd shy away from?

A. No.

Q. Are there any activities that have happened where you'd say, "Uh, oh," something is coming, and I know that it's going to reveal that I am unable to write something. Is writing a primary problem? Spelling and that sort of thing? Do you work hard at hiding your learning disability?

A. No one ever questions me about it. It doesn't come up. Now I have two brothers who are learning disabled, and I think it affects G——, my youngest brother. I don't know about D——. Yeah, I think to a certain extent I am not the same way as G——. G—— shies away from people a lot. D—— is more just a loner, not shy, he's just so overly aggressive that he scares people and sends them in kind of in opposite directions. But D—— is not socially all right. But I think G—— is more severe.

Q. Especially when you think about your brothers, both seem to have problems with socialization, and G—— may be much more noticeably (impaired).

A. Yeah, I would say so.

Q. And yet you are very confident about your social life and
    social skills. Do you have some reasons as to why you are
    different from your brothers and you've developed this
    confidence?

A. I don't know, perhaps I was able to succeed a little bit
    earlier academically than they did. And perhaps G——'s so-
    cial outlet was baseball and sports. He loves baseball and
    sports, and he concentrated on that. That is his area of
    success. I'm not sure about D——. Maybe work, he's kind
    of big on work. That's where he got his big chance. But
    everybody finished high school without any special educa-
    tion. But G—— did it through the, he ended up getting his
    high school diploma in the Marine Corps.

Q. So you think that your early academic success has led to a
    degree of confidence in yourself?

A. I think so. If I had to pin it on something, I'd say that was
    a positive factor.

Q. Would you say that you feel more comfortable in group
    settings opposed to one-to-one or close friends? Are you
    more comfortable in groups or would you like to go out on
    a one-to-one basis with another friend? Any difference in
    any feelings toward one situation versus the other that would
    be extraordinary from other non-learning-disabled people?

A. I had a lot of people that I knew and that I could socialize
    with in high school. Only a few who I considered real good
    friends. I don't like crowds in a Mardi Gras kind of crush.
    Large groups seem to be a little problem, but not when I
    lecture at the dental school. I find that more difficult than
    talking to a small group of students, six or seven students.
    I can talk very easily and talk to large groups. I feel like I
    need to prepare more. I don't do a lot of lecturing, and I've
    never asked anyone how they felt about that, but it's easier
    for me to talk to a small group, especially if there's
    interaction.

Q. If you're in a large reception or a social setting like that,
    do you have any problem tracking the conversation with a
    lot of people around you talking?

A. No, I'm real, real good auditorially, and in fact I attribute a lot of the success I've had to that. I think most of my problems were visual.

Q. I'd like to ask another kind of question now. And when I use the word effective, I really want you to focus on advantages stemming from your learning disability. Are there are any ways that in any way your learning disability would have been an advantage for you or make you more effective in your adult functioning?

A. The only positive thing I see to it is that I feel like I work pretty hard at anything that I do. It's probably because I've had to work so hard to do a lot of these things, and maybe if it had come easier, I wouldn't have stuck to it. I think not so much getting through high school. That was kind of a joke. But my undergraduate school and then dental school. I had to really hang in there, and I feel I worked pretty hard to get through. I'm finding since graduation that you still have to work very hard in this life, and I think some of my friends have just quit too soon, before they achieved what they wanted to. And that would be the positive side.

Q. Did it give you more of a sense of perseverance?

A. No, I just know that I have to work harder to accomplish.

Q. And when was that realization, early on?

A. I'd say about third grade.

Q. You just really knew that you had to dig in there for inner strength. Did you just realize it at that time?

A. Well, I also looked for shortcuts. I was good at them too.

Q. I don't want to interpret or project here, but I guess what you're saying is that you knew and know that you have to work harder, in fact that you've worked hard and succeeded. Does that give you a sense of confidence about yourself?

A. Yeah. I think if I could, if I can work, if I have the time to work at it, I can do it. I had several friends in high school who I felt were much brighter than I was, or at least academics were a lot easier for them. It took them until they were thirty-five to finish college, if they finished at all and that sort of thing. The thing I would say is that empathy and sensitivity got me through. I think that helped me gain sensitivity toward other people. I think a lot of that is important in education.

Q. One other question in this general area. Are your children aware of the concept of learning disabilities or of your difficulties stemming from your learning disabilities?

A. Yes. In fact, K—— has some difficulty. She's in the sixtieth percentile or above in school, but it hasn't been easy for her. She doesn't feel that her reading skills are what she wants them to be, and her language skills and math skills are up to par. We talked about it a lot because we had her tested. In the third grade, her visual perception was tested in school and all that stuff, and she was scored at kindergarten level at that time. We sat down and talked to her about it at that time, emphasizing all the time that you're a smart little girl. It's not difficult because you're not smart, it's difficult because you have some problems.

· Q. Tell me about your oldest daughter.

A. We've talked about that with her. Remembering from the past, we told her she had a problem. It wasn't an excuse that she could use to be poor at school. I think at one time she was kind of leaning on that a little bit. She told me recently she decided that she really is smart. It takes a while to come to that conclusion. I think you have to mature to a certain extent to say, "You know this guy really is dumb. Maybe I'm not so dumb, so bad off." To learn not so much your place, but where you fall. Her mother taught her a lot of study skills and, you know, strategies, and she learned confidence. The best thing that's happened recently is she and her friend both got their California Test of Basic Skills (CTBS) scores back, and she was looking at them realizing that she had scored higher than her friend in two areas. It doesn't do any harm to compare. I think it helped both of them. It really helped K——'s self confidence, and it helped me too.

Q. Do you ever feel that you have a special or unique ability to be able to understand your daughter?

A. Yeah, I think so. I can appreciate a lot of what she's going through academically. I think our experiences parallel quite a bit so far. She's a little bit ahead of me. She is reading real good for her age. In fact, she came to me a couple of weeks ago, and she said, "I know the only way to really build up my reading skills right now is to read, and I want to do as much reading as I can."

Q. I'd like to go into the area of emotional functioning and, again, please feel free to cast off anything that you're not comfortable with in our questioning. And as much as this may again seem very superficial, if you were to think of some adjectives, some words that would describe you emotionally, what are some words that come to mind?

A. General terms, maybe some apprehension, nervousness. I'm drawing a blank, now. Maybe, careful. Go on.

Q. Are you protective of yourself?

A. Yeah. I try to be pretty cautious. Tend not to take big risks.

Q. Has that involved part of your experience with and reaction to your learning disability at all?

A. Only in the sense that that's the way I approach my work, which demands being careful, and the way I approach study, reading.

Q. So it's a style that you have had to integrate within yourself, and that's something that works for you?

A. I think it probably was an expansion of, just of development. I guess, I'm trying to think of some other adjectives, tendencies that work for me. Some of this may be because I'm in the profession I'm in. I try not to be judgmental. I also think I am critical, critical sometimes. I think I am.

Q. Are you convinced about that?

A. Yeah, although it's hard for me to see myself like that. I still have to give that a lot of thought.

Q. I'd like to ask you some questions that are a little bit more direct.

A. I don't mind you asking more direct questions because I'm kind of floundering.

Q. That's understandable and, especially, it is hard because you are talking about emotions. How would you describe your self-esteem?

A. Self-esteem, I'd say I think a lot of myself. I don't feel like I'm the very best, but certainly not the least or less than the majority, and maybe that's the whole thing here. I see an awful lot of other people, and I don't have any problems with my self-esteem. That's why it's hard for me not to be judgmental. I try not to be critical of other people. I think maybe I am.

Q. Does it seem to make sense to you that you make judgments and perhaps even critical ones? Would it seem to make sense that you are still a fair person?

A. I tend not to comment one way or another until I have time to think about it, then going back to deliver it. I want to make sure that I'm understanding things really the way they are because I do realize I sometimes don't see things really as they are, and I want to make sure I do. I guess some people take that as being kind of a stuffed shirt at times, but it's just the way I have to be. I think my self-esteem has come a long way from second and third grades. It was tough to constantly fail at something I was expected to be very good at, and when you get in that cycle, it's hard to pull yourself out. It was still pretty bad until I got into college. I was taking my first biology course, and just studying harder than I'd ever studied before, and took the examination and made a "B." And the young lady that was sitting next to me commented that I must be very smart. That could be. Then when I went for the next class after that most of the auditorium was empty. I said yeah, I must be. (Laughing) And then there were some classes that I didn't succeed well in. Language, I'm very poor with. But then others I was good in, some of the science classes as an undergraduate taking graduate student sections. I'd be one of the top students in the class. So it kind of does this (motions up and down) because I have strengths in certain areas and weaknesses, and they don't level off very easily. My mother put me in kindergarten when I was four because she thought I was a problem learner, and then there were all kind of problems.

Q. Your time in college was a turning point?

A. Yes. It was continuous even through dental school until now.

Q. Are there any incidents along the way when all of a sudden something magical happened?

A. Yeah, until, the most dramatic thing that ever happened to me was one day when I looked at a picture and couldn't perceive what the picture was about. That was significant.

I couldn't explain it, what the picture was. It was a drum majorette with a baton in front of a band, and I guess it was second grade. And every day I'd come in and wonder what that damn picture was in front of the class. And I'd look at it, and I'd look at it and have no idea of what it was. It was just colors. It could have been modern art, just colors. They had no form, had no dimension. I could not begin to explain what it was. And then one day it clicked, and I was able to interpret what this picture was. And then I started to be able to interpret other paintings and photographs, some that I had grown up with around the house.

Q. Body language, facial expressions, and things like that. Would you have any problems interpreting those things back then before all the colors and forms and things made sense?

A. I really don't remember. I don't remember. Although I think I read body language pretty well. Maybe it's just because I'm in a profession now, and it's pretty easy to see. But that was dramatic. That's when I realized that something was wrong. Other people could appreciate these things, and I couldn't.

Q. Did that make you feel any way depressed or frustrated in any way?

A. Nah, I think I was just too young. It was just something that I realized. What really impressed me was the fact other kids in my class seemed to be able to read and understand these things on the page that I had no idea what they were or what was going on. And looking back, I can think about things and say, yeah, I had trouble with that because I couldn't figure it out. The teacher would draw a flower, then draw cats, and we had to paste them over her tracings, and looking down on them, place them in a scrapbook on a page everywhere. But I think I was too young to really have that kind of understanding. I knew I was having a hell of a time with it. I knew that the other kids weren't, that they seemed to be able to do a whole lot of things easier than I could. In school I was accused of a lot of things, daydreaming. Accused of not paying attention, being careless, so I tried, I just tried to be more careful and eventually I got it to where it was acceptable, the fact that it took a while. It was third grade, fourth grade before I could function in class.

Q. After third or fourth grade, were there any other times that you felt you were misunderstood by other people?

A. No, I always kind of looked at it as something I had to deal with. I didn't feel that people were misunderstanding me. I mean, I don't think I complained about it. I just tried to do things in different ways. Along about the seventh grade there were some other kids in the class that had probably more severe problems than I did, and if I would show them or work with them, they thought I was, "Hey, this guy knows his stuff," you know. Show them how to work with it and help them. I got a little success there. And then I guess the eighth grade I did pretty good. I had two teachers, and I don't think they are remarkable, I think that what they did helped me at the time. They both occurred in the eighth grade. One was a math teacher who just gave us a lot of problems, and we may have nine digit numbers that we would have to add and then we'd do a lot of subtraction. And I guess we did that for about twelve weeks, and by doing those exercises that rote, even though I hated it at the time, I got real good at following the columns and keeping my place. And then I had a reading teacher who had a workbook, and you would read and answer questions in a given moment, and I had a minute to read the paragraph. And with that I could see myself improving according to the grades you would make at the end. And I don't think he was a particularly good reading teacher or this guy was really a good teacher; I think he just managed to hit something in an area that I needed, working. And then after that I really had no problems, ninth grade through high school, except I was taking French, and I had a lot of trouble with that. But I went to a public high school, and a guy was reading a book there, and he said he knew people that got a college degree and a doctorate without reading the book he was reading. And I feel the same way. I don't believe that high school was really a challenge and it's something to go through.

Q. What was the name of your public high school?

A. J—— High School.

Q. So are you saying that if you didn't have perseverance, you wouldn't have learned to concentrate or be organized and focused? You more or less trained yourself?

A. Yeah. And I knew if I didn't pay attention, I wouldn't pass the grade, and my ambition was to pass. (Laughing) Actually, I didn't like school very much. Still not crazy about it.

Q. How about when you were going through adolescence? How would you describe your adolescence and/or your relationship with your peers in adolescence?

A. I think it was pretty typical. There were kids I had fights with and disagreements with, and kids I got along with. I can't see anything unusual about that. In ninth grade, I had considerable problems with adjusting, but our school districts were changed suddenly. I was suddenly placed in a rival school, and I had some troubles there. When I came, when I left O—— Parish and moved out here to K——, I wasn't thrilled with K—— Junior High School. I didn't like that. But other than those two incidents, I think I got along pretty well with kids.

Q. How about if we go back just a little bit to some of the more basic questions, such as when you feel most anxious, when you feel least anxious?

A. Most anxious has to be when I'm giving an injection. Least anxious when I'm fishing or gardening. If I can do a physical activity, that will take care of my anxiety.

Q. What do you think contributes most to stress or anxiety for you?

A. Money. (Laugh) No, actually, there are things that go with the territory in dentistry, and if you do dentistry long enough, you're going to have a problem with injections, and I haven't had any yet. Just stacking them against me. (Laughing) That's very hard for me. I don't enjoy that at all. Sometimes in what I do, I didn't realize it getting into it. It's not always, you know just, well, let's see how I can describe it. Sometimes you hurt the hell out of somebody, and there's nothing you can do about it, and you can prepare them for it and hope that they understand, but that doesn't

lessen the anxiety. I mean, it's not socially acceptable to
stick pins in people, you know, pull out teeth and worry
parents of kids. There was that little old lady this morning.
She was in there, and I was saying, "Oh, oh, oh I'm so
sorry, I'm so sorry. I'm really trying to do better. There's
just no way." She told me that it was the first time I hurt
her in ten years. I said, "I hope it's the last time." No, my
job produces a lot of anxiety in that realm ordinarily. I don't
think I'm excessively anxious. Normal things make me anxious. If I had to get up in front of a group and read something that I did not have a chance to go over, that would
be very anxious. Getting back to learning disability. And
even reading aloud, probably can be better than I can reasonably be if I have time to prepare. There are words that
I know are in my vocabulary, and I am not able to read
them. But oftentimes I read in the car (while a passenger),
and I have problems even when reading the light kind of
stuff.

Q. Do you feel a certain amount of stress even, say, in the car
   reading?

A. No, but if I had to do it in front of a group, white knuckles.
   About a fifty/fifty chance it would be a rather embarrassing
   time. I mean, you know, a doctor should know these things.

Q. Do you have anything to add before we move on to another
   area of the interview?

A. Yes, I think my brother has gone pretty far despite himself.
   He is doing some contracting, subcontracting, and he does
   a lot of good work. From what I've seen, it seems to be
   pretty good, but he questions himself. I think it pretty much
   blows away your ego. His parents still treat him like he's
   retarded. Yeah. He came to my wife after he was in the
   Marine Corps, and she didn't appreciate what he was saying.
   He brought to her the Marine Corps manual, which we got
   that day, and he said, "You see this book, I read this book."
   She said, "Oh, yeah, fine." But I can appreciate what he
   was saying. To him this was like climbing Mt. Everest. I
   mean, he made it to the top. He read one book in his life,
   you know, and I think D— is a little bit more of a reader

than G——. G—— will probably never read another book in his life. But he read that one.

Q. Did it surprise you when you realized what he was saying?

A. This might make a difference to people like that. And I realize there are different levels of learning disabilities, and mine may not be as severe as some, maybe not as severe as my brothers'. But I still don't read fiction. Well, about every five years I do. I don't read for pleasure, I read to get information.

Q. I've asked this question before, let's get back to the topic. What are some of the factors that contribute to you being more successful than your brother?

A. I was probably pushed harder as firstborn, and I mean the whole family just knew I was a genius. I had to be, and I think they expected a lot of success, and I tried to provide it. And then me trying to please, I just realized I had to work pretty hard at it, and it feels pretty good to have accomplished some things. With my hyperactivity too.

Q. Are you surprised that you are a dentist?

A. I was until I got into dental education. There are some things that I'm very good with as well as abstract reasoning. These little tests where they have these figures that are unfolded, spatial relationships. I can eat those things up, and I don't know why. If it's not visual, it's not much trouble. If you put three things in one or four things in one and slightly different, I probably could not pick it out. But if you show me something unfolded and say, "What would it look like if it were folded," I can tell you what it would look like when you fold it up. And that was the part of the dental aptitude test, and I did very well on that.

Q. Did you carve chalk in your exam?

A. I did carve chalk and no problems at all. It was chalk carving and abstract reasoning and other things. Some of my strong points.

Q. Had you done any work before that led you into dentistry or do any jobs related to dentistry? Or did you say all of a sudden, "Dentistry!"

A. No, I went into engineering because all of the testing that

I had taken in high school and before always pointed in the direction of being an engineer. And I decided engineering was the pits. And I was taking a biology course, and that wasn't too bad. And I got to thinking about that and the fact that I wasn't going to ever become an engineer, and I said, "What can you do with a degree in biology," and I said, "Nothing." And I thought about what might be close. And there was medicine, which was the closest thing, medicine and dentistry, veterinary medicine. I was in junior division wanting to be a dentist or a physician. No way was I going to become a veterinarian, looked into dentistry, so I kind of set that as a goal and even thought that perhaps that was out of reach at the time. But I said, well, I'll try for it. Stay out of the draft for Vietnam. (Laughing) And so I found out there was this aptitude test, and it was coming up. And I signed up for that at the last minute, and I only took it once, and I certainly did well enough on it to be accepted into dental school. And then as far as applying, my wife talked me into applying and said something like, "You can't get accepted if you don't send in an application." So I did that. It's her fault I'm a dentist. (Smile)

Q. You didn't go to dental school in Louisiana did you?
A. No.
Q. In Maryland?
A. Maryland, not in D.C. By time, my folks were living in Maryland, and so I had to find schools in that area. I did apply to other southern schools. L——was accepting thirty people out of state. And at that time, I wrote to Georgia and Alabama and if you were out of state, just forget about it. I had this feeling that once I got into it, I could just get past the academic part. I could get accepted and get through that first couple of years with all those med. students in my classes.
Q. What do you mean the first couple of years?
A. Basic courses like anatomy and the pharmacology.
Q. Did you feel that you were physically prepared for what you had to do? As a dental student?
A. Yeah. I did what I had to do. I'd get home and study about as long as I could and then hope for the best. The curriculum

was a combined curriculum with the dental students, the medical students, and the postgraduate students all taking the same courses and all tested in the same tests, same auditorium, same grade. And it was pretty tough, but there were so many there, and I always just stayed at least in the middle.

Q. What did you do for your writing abilities?

A. No problem. Multiple choice tests.

Q. Tell me about issues related to writing and testing.

A. The only problems I ever had with that were the instructors who would give you the name of someone and you'd put it down a couple of times with a slightly different spelling, and that was a bit confusing. I remember my studying in short spurts of time. I remember getting home and studying in intervals and trying to do something in between to break the monotony. But ten or fifteen minutes of really concentrated studies, and that was about as much as I could stand and then stop it. When I get tired, my eyes get tired. I don't know whether it's something that's just a borderline thing or something that only happens when I'm tired. They couldn't pick it up unless they tested me when I am really tired. But you can look at me and see one eye going in a different direction, not working with the other one anymore. So it was a real concentrated effort to be able to focus the eyes together, in about fifteen-minute stretches. I would read fifteen minutes and take a few minutes off to rest my eyes and go back to it.

Q. So therefore being in a dental practice is a piece of cake in comparison to being in dental school.

A. (Pause) I wouldn't say dental practice is a piece of cake.

Q. Let me clarify for you. Because of the pressure of passing tests and intense studying. Perhaps there's more pressure in practice, rather than making the grade and being on top of the material?

A. Yeah. In that sense, I've got a terrific memory, and once it gets in there, it don't get out, so I don't have to go back. I can usually follow through and pick up what I need as far as physiology and pharmacology or whatever while I'm doing the treatment or what treatment service to prescribe.

Fortunately, most things in dentistry are routine. I have reasonable ability with my hands, and I can pretty much make them do what needs to be done. So, yeah, from the technical aspects, dentistry is a piece of cake. Once I got to the clinic and the really challenging academic work was behind me, I had no problems.

Q. I'm wondering if your wife helped you in your studies while going through your dental education.

A. In some areas, yeah. Obviously, she couldn't help me with the physics and chemistry. In undergraduate school, we took a lot of courses together—mostly electives. And whenever we took electives, we studied together.

Q. I don't mean this in a negative sense, but could you have done it without your wife's support?

A. Except for German. I'd say with the exception of the German. She couldn't help me with that.

Q. You mentioned academic support, but how about any psychological support?

A. There was a speech course that she helped me a lot, but I was there before she came, and I was doing okay for myself.

Q. I would like to ask a few more questions, and I will try to be very specific. They are mostly open ended. In twenty-five words or less, if possible, what do you find satisfying about your profession?

A. I think it's the most satisfying thing. Number one, making a patient pleased with the product, with what I do, and then the satisfaction of doing it well. I can do good dentistry, and that's pleasing to me. And then the patient recognizing my efforts in being relieved of pain, and that's very gratifying. The patient comes in with pain, and I make him feel fantastic. Secondly, when they come, I usually do a pretty good job for them.

Q. Do you see any ways in which your learning disabilities affect you professionally now?

A. Yeah. I do not have much trouble working backward in the dental mirrors, I don't have much problem with that.

Q. To yourself, do you relate to that?

A. Yeah, I think that's a real plus. You know, doing intricate work with direct vision is one thing. Doing intricate work through a mirror is something else, and I'm probably pretty good at that. And maybe because I do sometimes see things backward.

Q. How about professional/academic writing?

A. Then there is publishing. I can jump in there and write. But it's not particularly easy. Not so much because I don't know what I'm talking about, just that it's very difficult to look at that blank page. While I see others at the dental school, I easily add some things five, six, seven times. You know I go through it, and a few times it's just trying to find grammatical errors. One of my colleagues at work pretty much taught me how to write all this. Real logical ways to organize or whatever. In my first years in undergraduate school, my writing was just dreadful. Now I write much better. Also, my wife and I have sort of skills complementing skills, and we help each other. She helps me, and I help her with the writing for her jobs.

Q. I'd like to close out the vocational section by asking you a question you may have answered in a variety of ways. I think one thing in this area which we have talked about is how learning disabilities may have influenced your choice of profession. You said you chose dentistry over medicine, etc.

A. (Before question was finished) I didn't realize it was more difficult. I would say by the time I reached L——, I had gotten out of the junior division, the only professions that held any mystique were in the area of medicine and dentistry. I couldn't think of anything else that I would have had an interest in pursuing through future study. I take that back. Electron physics would have been more interesting, but would have been a problem for me. I had some friends who "play in that ball game," but it varies. But those things that you think of, I would have felt confident of, I think I would have been a good geologist or a good teacher or a good engineer. Couldn't have been a good English major, couldn't have done that.

Q. Let's take it one step further. If you had never had any kind of learning disabilities, would you have had the same career choice?

A. Oh, I don't know. I don't know. That's been with me for
so long that I was, because of my learning disabilities, I
knew that I better stick with something that all this testing
of people who were smarter than me telling you what to do.
Well, when your area is science and engineering, you better
stick with science and engineering. Those are where your
talents lie, so I figured you better go with your talents. I
wasn't going to try English literature because, I mean, that
just was like a foreign language. I had no illusion about
those things, but as far as getting into college and overcoming your low-level courses, I didn't have any fear of that
once I was in there. The first year, I was scared to death
because I didn't know what to expect. Friends were dropping
out like flies. Everybody was leaving. Why am I still here?
I'd better keep doing what I've been doing. After I was
there for a while, I had plenty of confidence to do whatever
I wanted to do. Dentistry might have been more than I
really thought to do. Once I got in, I'm not surprised that
I got through. My dad was very friendly with the dean at
a university in Washington, D.C., and Dad set an appointment at that university. He said apply there. You can't get
accepted there if you don't apply there. And I felt that I
probably would be accepted, but I didn't want to be at the
bottom of the class if I were accepted because the dean and
my dad were friendly. I didn't want that, so I didn't do that.
But, I knew that if I could be accepted on my own merit,
that I could get through it. One way or another, I would
get through it. Does that answer it?

Q. We've talked a lot about the vocational area. That has also
yielded lots of information about your education. If you
want to add anything about your educational experiences
that are important and we haven't talked about yet, then
we can do it now. Just to be more specific, were you ever
labeled "learning disabled" while in school?

A. No.

Q. People had an idea that you were having some problems?

A. Oh, I had a lot of tutoring. I think my parents really felt
something was out of kilter, you know, after they got past
the idea that I wasn't really a genius. They still appreciated

that there was something wrong and well maybe he needs a little help with reading skills. And I had a lot of tutoring, both family and privately.

Q. That's about the only question that I see that we didn't cover.

A. I think really nobody knew what was going on at that point and time. My brother G——, who is about eight years younger than me, his problems were severe enough to where they decided to have him tested. And when he was first tested, they said, "Well, he's retarded." If you met my brother G——, you would realize that, while he wasn't Einstein, he was certainly not retarded. Not even a slow learner.

Q. It seems apparent to me that you are very independent with daily, routine things. But can you tell me more? Can you tell me about driving, about managing your money, and things like shopping? Do you cook? Do you have problems with instructions? Do you have problems being on time, finding places around town?

A. Wait, yes.

Q. Finding places around town, maps, giving and following directions?

A. Giving directions and following directions; I say go right when I mean turn left. Instructions, too, like putting things together. I'll take things out of the box and start getting the pieces together instead of reading the instructions. And if I read the instructions, I still don't understand the instructions. My wife can read them to me, and I'm fine. If she reads the instructions to me, I'll get it assembled. If I have to read the instructions, I'll be half the day reading the instructions.

Q. How about when you pack your clothes for vacations? Can you judge how much clothes you're taking or packing?

A. No problem with that.

Q. How about getting keys in locks, etc.? Any problems or complaints?

A. No problem.

Q. How do you deal with leisure time? Do you need leisure activities to be structured?

A. Yes. I try to make it that way. I go out of my way to. I'm the world's greatest piddler. I go off and try to do something and not really worry about whether or not it gets done or leave it half done, whatever. I try to overcome that. If I'm working, I am so scheduled with working that I try to ease up. If I have a day off, I'll try not to even look at the clock. So I just do that. I don't have any problems with unstructured time. In fact, I'd rather be a bum. Can you imagine a person asking, "What do you want to be when you grow up?" and I say a bum. Dr. Bum. (Laugh)

Q. I'm interested when you first became aware of the term "learning disabilities."

A. Well, I guess while my wife and I were dating. She would talk about these interesting things, and I'd say, "Hey, that applies to me." Or I would say, "do this," and she'd say, "Yeah, you're LD." Before that, I knew there was, you know, something different, but, you know, I didn't have anything to blame. It was just there, and I didn't know about it. Obviously, I didn't read about it. Probably could have gone on, perhaps never understanding it. Just I would have known that it was there.

Q. What is your reaction to learning disabilities in past years?

A. I was surprised to find that I had a history teacher that actually admitted to reading numbers in the wrong order. It was common for me, and I thought it was just something unique to me. And then this was in high school, and he said he did it too, and I said, "That's interesting, he got through college. I guess I can." Again, the most dramatic thing for me was when I was able to interpret what things I was looking at, what they really were, letters, pictures, whatever, just symbols, couldn't have put them together.

Q. This realization of your learning disability and an understanding of what it was, did it change your outlook on life?

A. Yeah. It made me think that for the first time the world wasn't just divided up into smart people and dumb people and that I wasn't on the dumb side. I think I always felt like I was street smart, but that somehow I was conning my way through school. When I started understanding about being LD in that sense, it made one look at things a little bit different. I was taking a course in college, and there was another man who was taking courses with me who was very very bright, and I always looked up to him as one of the brightest people I knew. And this man graduated at the top of his class with a perfect 4.0 average, very bright.

Q. Valedictorian?

A. Yes, I've always done very well academically. Test for test, every test that we took together, I scored better than he did, and it used to drive J—— up the wall. But I would come home and (laugh). That was one of the best confidence-building things that I've had over the years. It finally kind of convinced me, I think, that it wasn't a matter of being street smart but really that I had good analytical skills and that I was really bright. And it was academics that more than anything else specifically that gave me problems.

Q. This is something that we've talked a little bit about already, but I will ask you again. You are successful by many standards. I understand that you are a very successful professional, and you have much to be very proud of. So this question could be asked of anyone, but especially it concerns you probably because you had to work a lot harder to get where you are. What do you think are the reasons for your success?

A. Perseverance. Really. That's all. I truly believe that if you give anybody enough time, they will eventually graduate from high school, college. No, I think that's all that matters. Just perseverance. That's what I see, and I don't believe that it's a great deal different with your graduate students or undergraduates. If you will allow them enough time to work it through, and if they have the desire, and if they are a capable person, they will get through.

Q. Perseverance is one thing that is central to your success and incrementally you have always been able to build success. Will you trace your successes for me?

A. Yeah, I could probably outline them for you. Kindergarten, first grade, second grade, sixth grade were exceedingly tough for me, and I wondered whether or not I would get through them. Some courses at L—— were almost devastating for me. German was tough, and I thought I would probably have to redo that. I did have to redo some like German.

And there were other classes. There was a math course that I just barely got through. Those two were really tough. But they were all successes because I passed them. I learned, I would take notes, and then I would use the notes with the reading and fill in my notes and fill in my reading with the notes. But if I heard the notes, if I heard the instructor I had the notes, and sometimes I would have to read something maybe four times to grasp what was being said. And this is difficult when you are doing it in ten- to fifteen-minute time slots. I usually did much better if the course work wasn't so much reading but more math or formulations, and because it's that way in chemistry and physics. I did real well with balancing the equations and doing the math.

Q. That's all the questions. You've really done an amazing job. You've covered just about everything we hoped you would. Thanks so much for your time.

Interview with S7

Q. I would like to begin by asking some very specific and simple questions. I may write some answers down. And once we get past some few very general basic questions, I probably won't write at all. Please don't feel nervous. Just answer the questions as fully as you wish. The interview is being audiotaped, as you know. So that will allow for a conversation-like format. Please remember that we respect your privacy and don't wish to make you uncomfortable by asking questions you don't want to answer.

Q. You said you're thirty-three years old?

A. Yes, thirty-three.

Q. You are married?

A. Not married.

Q. Have you ever been married?

A. No.

Q. And this is your mother's home?

A. It's her home since my dad passed away. If something happens to her, it comes to me.

Q. Are you presently employed?

A. Not at this moment. I haven't been for, since 1983.

Q. Do you have a high school diploma?

A. Yes, I guess you can call it a diploma with learning disabilities. With my problem and everything, my mother searched out the United States to see if there was any place to send me, and the only place for that was in Texas at B—— Remedial Clinic. It was especially for kids with dyslexia and learning disabilities. Not physical, but sometimes I guess it got physical after years in school when they didn't know about dyslexia. And they were ridiculed or teased, and then it became a physical handicap. You know, mental, psychological, some hyperactive, and, you know, overweight, and this is a psychological aspect of dyslexia. And some developed because of, I guess, some physical illness. They weren't retarded, but they were just slow in reading.

Q. Didn't you graduate from a high school in the greater New Orleans area?

A. No. While I was there, they enrolled me into a correspondence course called A—— School of C——. Through the clinic, they helped me through the courses, the reading parts.

Q. Where did you go to school?

A. I went to the clinic. I went to L—— School and the surrounding schools here in New Orleans. They couldn't do anything for me because it was public so I went to M—— C——, where they knew about it. They helped me as much as they could, but still didn't do any good. Then S—— School, then someone suggested that I went to M—— School, and my mama jerked me out of there as quick as she could. There was a lot of kids there that were (no retrieval of words). I said, "Hey mom, I don't belong here."

Q. In what year was this? Was it around 1965?

A. No.

Q. 1968, something like that. You went to M—— School?

A. Yeah.

Q. The time when you would have been around high school age.

A. I think it was about thirteen when I went to Texas.

Q. Was that about 1966?

A. They had kids there from all over the United States, Air Force kids, and service children. New Orleans started it off when it spun off into two schools there, R—— School and B—— R—— Clinic, which was a spin-off.

Q. When you were there, you were a teenager in high school. Were you aware of a term called learning disabilities?

A. Well, I think that's what they called it.

Q. Is that what they were calling it at that time? Or were they calling it dyslexia instead of learning disabilities at that time?

A. I don't remember what they were calling it. They were aware of learning disabilities, yeah, if you want to call it learning disabilities. But they taught you how to function with it. You learn some.

Q. Let's change the line of questioning a little bit. What are your interests, your hobbies, and what kinds of things do you like to do?

A. I have a clear interest in entertaining, like singing or playing drums or something to do with entertaining. I still try to play, but there's not too many people around to just play.

Q. Do you do that now? What are your interests like now? The kind of things that you like to do and enjoy doing with your time?

A. I like playing music and doing a lot of church work. I do a lot of helping people out.

Q. Through your church?

A. Through my church, like going on mission with teams. Work projects throughout the world, wherever.

Q. So have you been out of New Orleans helping out in different regions or areas?

A. Last year we went to France. Our church had a team go to France to work on a project there. That's the reason I am unemployed. Before that, I took off to go to Costa Rica for three weeks. When I came back, the job was already filled, so I looked for other work. The job that I had was driving a truck, and there wasn't much future in it. I am seeking to better my skills, ministering or helping people out.

Q. Do they do work in the New Orleans area as well?

A. We have, not work projects. But they have like campus crusades and other missionary groups that focus on certain salvation in our ministry. What I do is get involved meeting somebody on the side to share with. It was a minister who helped me like that.

Q. It sounds like you do a lot of work in the church. Anything besides the drums, music, and the church? Anything that you like to do in your spare time? I heard you used to have model trains. Are you still pursuing that or anything else?

A. It sort of, it goes in the attic for right now. It takes up a lot of room. You can get caught up in a lot of time with that stuff. I've got a lot of other things that's more important.

Q. Well, S7, it sounds like you do a lot of different things and do a lot of traveling to help with problems for the church. Is there something that you would think of as a typical day for you? Not so much when you are traveling or doing a special project with the church, but could you describe just a normal every day for you?

A. Well, lately, I get up. These last few months I have been sort of taking it easy, keep the house, yard, and everything. But I really haven't, except for the church work. It's the only other activity that I've been really doing at the time. A regular day when nothing is going on, I just sort of float along. It's kind of hard to describe each day, specifically.

Q. On any given day you might be doing something with the church?

A. I get kind of concerned because you know my abilities aren't really. I know how to do a lot of things, but they are not enough, nothing that I can support myself on. I do a little cooking, here at home, or whatever you call it, and do a little woodworking, a little yard work, sort of helping out. And not being able to accomplish a lot with my problem, you know, you just kind of discouraged and sit back and sometimes sort of fall into a mood where I just don't feel like doing anything.

Q. What puts you in that mood?

A. Lack of, you know, accomplishment, you know. I call it blah, but not enough to set new priorities. I have a problem expressing myself so when you are talking to people who don't have the problem, you know, it's kind of hard to have conversations with other people.

Q. So, for instance, if you were in sales or an occupation like that, you'd think that other people would judge you as not expressing yourself well? You think that would be a problem as far as selling or meeting the public? Was that ever a problem when you were driving your truck?

A. Well, not really because I didn't, all I did was pick up and deliver. The only time I saw other people was when unloading and loading.

Q. Are you comfortable in talking with that job?

A. If you were to sell something or, leadership, you know, but I see other people with my problem and history. They have such success out of what course they took. They probably didn't know they had it, so it wasn't a weakness, you know. They were forced to make do with what they had and not feel that because I know I have dyslexia, I guess I sort of make excuses for myself, you know. I can't do that because I'm too slow. You know? I am too slow.

Q. Do you feel that you are making excuses for yourself or do you feel that you should stay away from some of these jobs?

A. Sometimes I am. I don't like to say I'm a quitter, you know, I don't like to quit, you know. I've just learned to say, "What the heck," you know.

Q. Well, S7, I think as you know from talking with P—— that the purpose of what we're doing is to talk to adults about how they are coping with the world. For you, some of the things that you do and what you're involved in. As we talk, it seems that you're saying that you're not entirely satisfied with everything about your life. At the same time, as I look at it, it seems that there are some very good things about your life too. You are taking care of yourself in a lot of ways. You obviously can take care of yourself to a great extent. So I'm interested as much as anything else in how you take care of yourself and what ways that you do that. But I think it also might be important for our discussion to think of how your learning disabilities affect you in your adult life, and that is what we have been talking about. It may not always be a problem, and even in some cases, there might be some good things that come from having learning disabilities. Now I would just like to ask some very general questions about different parts of being an adult. Let's focus on your social life, what you do for recreation and friends, including the church if you wish. Could you tell me, how you would describe your social life and some of the things that you do socially?

A. At the present time, my social life is kind of bleak right now. I don't, I did go to, sort of had a social life at M——. I did have a social life there and friends there. Just a few guys, but really I just stuck to myself. Everybody was working, and when they are at home, I'm working or doing something. I guess it seems like their schedule doesn't coordinate with mine or mine doesn't coordinate with them. I try to keep an open social life with my relatives and family as much as I can. At this time, my social life is sort of kind of bleak.

Q. Could you tell me something about some of your family affairs and how much you get together with your family? Also what are some of the things you do?

A. Mainly eat together. It's about the only time we see each other. Or P—— will come over with his family from across the lake, and we sometimes do things with each other and, of course, they are leading their lives and are not around as plentiful as, you know, as much as we may want to. I've gone to some Bible studies and made a social life out of that, you know. Meeting other people and having conversations and going on outings with them, I guess. Most of my social life is based around family and church activities.

Q. What are some of the kinds of church activities that you attend? You said, for instance, you get together for Bible readings?

A. Bible studies, picnics, I go to the zoo sometimes. I go for fun. It's nothing like a date situation. It's more just like a social or just a get-together. When we go on mission teams, we go together and do things together. Not just work all the time but have fellowship in that way. We go bowling sometimes, just, you know, fellowship.

Q. Do you feel comfortable with your social life and with your friends in the church?

A. Yeah, because their intellect is more, a little higher than mine. Not all of them are slowed down with speech or sort of toned down. I guess with my problem, I'm not as quick with words as they are. So it sort of separates, you know, people with higher intellect.

Q. It's not an issue is it?

A. No, they are very accepting. It's just the way you feel. The way everything mixes together. It seems to me, I remember we used to talk, you know, it seems like they had some really nice people at the church and nice fellowship. Of course, they have their problems too, and they come and go. Nobody stays together. You have moments. You have days when you're doing everything with them and days when you are not seeing each other. And you sort of grow in and grow out of it. There's nothing like a romance right now or a man-woman relationship. I try to look for a similar moral standard as I have. Ladies of the evening are not the answer. I hope I'm answering this all right.

Q. You're doing fine.

A. I could ramble on, you know.

Q. That's fine. How about some close friends? Do you have a couple male close friends or guys from high school days or the neighborhood that you are close with?

A. Not really anymore. We just sort of drifted away. A couple of guys from the clinic, that we went to school together with. And they sort of went their way, drifted apart. I don't know if that's normal or what, but that's the way it happened. Sometimes in life people go different directions.

Q. I find that in my life that I've come close and drifted apart too. But would you say you make friends easily?

A. Yeah, I guess so. I guess my problem . . . I guess I'm basically shy. I'm scared of rejection or, you know, sort of conscious of how I present myself. Sometimes I have a problem I come on too strong or not strong enough or first impression is not always the true impression. After you get to know them, and then you get to know them because the first impression is sometimes a cover-up, you know, from the way you really present yourself. You get to know somebody, then you find out how they really are.

Q. Do you find that it's a little uncomfortable for you when you are meeting people for the first time?

A. Yeah. I'm friendly, I shake their hand and everything, and

I greet them. But then it gets past knowing each other, it gets beyond courtesy.

Q. Are there times when you feel comfortable talking to people? In terms of expressing yourself, are there situations when you are comfortable with that?

A. When I first talk (laugh), I guess I'm limited in my speech. It's what I say or think to say. I run out of things to say. I don't know if it's lack of reading or with reading problems, I can't hit on other people's ideas. I could be wrong. What they had us doing at school was writing a story, a long story. That sort of helped us to forget. Just writing, just about something, a story or write something. I think they did that so we could project our own ideas and thoughts. It helped us.

Q. Do you feel that when you meet people or even when you're just talking to people, that they are going to be aware that you have some learning problems?

A. I think so. I guess that's why I'm shy. I don't know how they conceive of me or if I'm able to understand what they say.

Q. Everybody in your family knows that you have a learning problem, right?

A. Yeah.

Q. How about your nieces and nephews? How do you interact with them? Are they good relationships?

A. Oh yeah, I guess it is. They have their own interests. I try to be friendly with them, have a relationship. They're at an age where they are choosing their own paths now, and we're not as close to them as I was.

Q. How old is your nephew?

A. He's eleven, I think, eleven, twelve.

Q. And then P——'s oldest is a girl?

A. A girl.

Q. How old is she?

A. Nine or ten.

Q. They are getting older.

A. Yeah. They are having their struggles too. I don't know if any of them have a learning disability yet. I haven't found out. M—— is a genius.

Q. He's a smart kid.

A. He has a high IQ. Of course, some kids with learning disabilities have a high IQ too, but getting it here to here is a
   problem, then here to here. They call it "expressaphasia"
   or something, what they call it. That's what they diagnosed
   me as.

Q. Well, shall we move on to another part of the interview? I
   would just like to follow up one question, and I want to
   make this an open-ended question. Do you feel more comfortable with people if they know that you have learning
   disabilities, or would you prefer that people don't know that?

A. I like to be honest if they are depending on me to behave
   in a normal way. I'd like them to know the reason that I'm
   slow, not as an excuse, but I just like to be open. Let them
   know up front, then they know what to expect. I don't like
   to use it as an excuse, but I just like them to understand
   why I'm not as fast as somebody else.

Q. In your church group, do your friends there know that you
   have learning disabilities?

A. I think some of them do. My pastor and minister do. They
   know of my problem. I just let them know flat out. I'm
   good at physical labor. They don't require too much reading
   or too much math or thought. This is keeping with my
   problem. I've more ability in my hands. I'm good at ham-
   mering, but figuring out the sizes is hard for me, and I guess
   that's what the problem is. Having the kind of job you gotta
   know mathematics and gotta read and all that stuff. Been
   trying to find careers that don't involve all that stuff, but
   can't get by without it. If Rockefeller can do it, he had a
   million dollars to fall back on. I couldn't do any of this
   without my faith in Christ. He has blessed me with family
   who understand, friends who understand and has been most
   gracious and most helpful in my spiritual life and just sort
   of kept me in view of reality. I often fall back on His way,
   the kingdom of God and righteousness and all these things
   shall be added unto you. It stays in my mind all the time,
   you know. As long as I'm serving Him and myself, give
   myself to Him, He is going to supply my needs and that's
   the only reason I'm able to make it today. I guess because
   of my handicap, I am aware of it, and it draws me closer

to the Lord. All I have for Him, He's made it all to me. Through relationships with you and the people at church and other people who are understanding, most understanding about it. I feel sorry for people who are out there and who don't know Christ or the Lord. I couldn't handle anything without it. I think I noticed that when I was at the remedial clinic why He created me so slow. It must be for some reason or something in it for Him. I owe Him for my success that I do have, but it's nothing of myself. I've seeked training through all kinds of schools from here to Florida and from Texas to Florida to here. And things I've found out, I couldn't have accomplished any of it if it wasn't for the fact of the Lord, the faith to stick it out. No matter what.

Q. So you do think you are a person who works really hard at it, and you do stick with it? Or would you say that you are a person that gives up easily? Or a mixture? Where do you see yourself?

A. When I'm in myself, I give up. When I find the Lord's will, I accomplish a lot.

Q. So that gives you a lot of strength?

A. I couldn't do it without it. I get depressed sometimes when I'm away from the Lord. The Bible talks about that. Gives you high moments and low moments, you know. When you feel the world is coming on top of you. And then times when you're with the Lord, and you feel like you can conquer the world, sort of balance that out to accomplish what you're going to do.

Q. We better move on just a little bit. That bridges the gap. You're talking about times when you feel like the world is on top of you and other times it's easier. The first area that we talked about was social. Now we would like to talk about emotional things, then we will go to vocational and academic areas to ask questions. Can you think of words that would describe you emotionally? How do you think of yourself emotionally? What kinds of words do you think accurately describe you?

A. Run that question by me again.

Q. In an emotional sense, what do you think are some words

that describe you, your emotional state? You have conveyed thoughts of depression, but typically how do you feel, and how do you approach the world in the way you see yourself? Are you generally a happy person, a content person, or are you frustrated, are you depressed, are you angry, do you get very stressed, do you experience lots of anxiety?

A. At times I feel a lot of that. At different times, I feel stressful. Sometimes aggravated, angry, sometimes I feel, when I'm feeling good about myself, I feel successful.

Q. What makes you feel good about yourself? And then we'll ask you what makes you feel bad about yourself?

A. I feel good about myself because I'm able to overcome my handicaps, and sometimes I can't add up two and two, which is discouraging.

Q. When you overcome your learning disability, what are some examples of when you feel really good about yourself?

A. For instance, do yard work and do a good job. I sit back, and it looks good. Again when I'm going, when I do like woodworking, and I'm working on a project there and I do figuring. I keep making mistakes, and I get depressed. So I'm lacking in perseverance. My way to put it.

Q. Does it depend on the project, for instance? Do you persevere in the yard because you know you can do it, but you won't persevere in the woodworking because you know it's problem after problem after problem? So you know what you can and can't do?

A. I know my weak points and my strong points.

Q. When do you feel relaxed? How do you relax?

A. I feel relaxed after praying about my problem, feel relaxed with the Lord. It takes all the guilt and all the stress off. I feel good about myself when I do my daily devotional. No matter what happens, it really doesn't . . . it's nothing to worry about, it's just me and myself.

Q. You say you feel very relieved after you pray, and you get a load off your mind. Do you find, for instance, that in a stressful day, that you find yourself praying more than on other days and that it always helps you?

A. It helps me cope with problems and how to get on with life. I guess I get concerned because Mother won't be there all my life, and I may have to go on my own, earn my own living. And it makes me concerned on how I'm going to do that.

Q. So you worry about that?

A. In order for me to make a living for myself, I have to have success of something. I am concerned about that.

Q. Anything else?

A. Daddy, he was a workaholic. He was good at what he did, and he was sharp in math and all that other stuff. My abilities are limited to labor type work, nothing more. Not like reading or a lot of reading, or projecting myself or selling something.

Q. Let me jump ahead a little bit. When you think about what you might have to do to take care of yourself and support yourself, are there specific things that you think about?

A. How to support myself, maintain a house, and be productive, and how to offer the world something out of myself. And how to contribute to the world, to my part of the world, help others, and a family life. If some day should I have a family, how could I support them? Or if it's just me I could only support, and thoughts like that.

Q. You said earlier that sometimes thinking about the future caused you to be concerned. Are there any times when you feel good thinking about the future? Any strong points in yourself?

A. I find myself in whatever I'm a success at. If I can accomplish whatever, for instance, if I could go out and learn to play the drums and go out and play for others and be a success at something like that. Being a success in something like that.

Q. You told us very clearly some of the things that make you feel anxious and frustrated. However, when you are feeling good about yourself, do you see certain strong points about yourself? Do you see good qualities in yourself?

A. Good results. In whatever I accomplish, I feel good about myself. I really haven't thought a lot about it.

Q. Well, if I were to ask if you think of yourself as a nice person or as a not nice person, what would you see yourself as?

A. I would see myself as a nice person. Because what I'm going through, and in the past, I have some confidence in myself in what I've accomplished. I think I have accomplished a lot, but there's a lot more I need to accomplish. Like a light at the end of the tunnel, seems like you just about get there, but someone's always adding an extension to the tunnel.

Q. You constantly have to go further?

A. Yeah. That's it.

Q. Did you feel that way earlier on too? Did you constantly feel that the light is always there, you see it, but you never get closer to it?

A. I remember that feeling when I was a little boy. I would play like I was driving a truck. I had the same feeling.

Q. That was your most recent job before you went to Costa Rica? Correct?

A. Yeah. When I graduated, when I finished high school, I came out and Daddy entered me into the community college, in the rehab center to try and get me into some kind mechanics, auto mechanics. And I was going through that, and the mechanics school class was filled up. So I waited in the meanwhile. I was going through the remedial training, reading, math, and stuff, and the only classes they were able to put me in at the time was cooking and ceramics. So I just went in there to try it out. I guess I got bored at that, and then someone told me about heavy construction school in Miami out of H——, Florida, that would train me to operate heavy equipment. So I went through that and then entered like a five-week course. I learned to operate some equipment, but after I graduated, I found out that the school wasn't a reputable place. And I tried to get a job, and after I graduated, I wasn't able to get hired wherever I went to apply for a job. My uncle worked in the Florida rock mines, and I was able to get on a job there. Labor, and I worked with that for about three months. And after I finished there, then I came home and got a job with the Louisiana Road Department. And I remained there, where I got involved in delivering. And then my uncle in Florida again tried to get me on the road department there. So I went back there and had a short job for about less than a week. You know, it was just back and forth and in my career, and the last job that I had with M——'s Plywood was the longest I'd worked for five years.

Q. You worked for a couple of years, right?

A. Five years, and then this mission thing came up, and I went on it. And then that job closed down. And then at the present time, I haven't worked since.

Q. Do you want to work?

A. Yeah and no, on a, I want to establish some more careers or other abilities, entertaining or some kind of more mental work or something I can do.

Q. As opposed to physical?

A. There's not too much thought to drive a truck, you know. I want something where I can better myself.

Q. When you were driving, you did that for a number of years?

A. Five years.

Q. Were there things about driving a truck or having that job that you found satisfying?

A. Yeah. At the time, I was able to drive this big truck, and I was able to control it, and I drove it pretty good. Able to get around places and after a while, I learned to do more and was more able, and it got too simple.

Q. Did you have the same route or same deliveries? Did you go out of town?

A. It varied. It was in town, local, and in parts of South Louisiana. And it was delivering for the company and picking up customers. And then it wasn't satisfying when it got to be for five years. And after I, after five years there, I guess I'd achieved as far as I could go with them. And when I got involved in church, they were more "holy" and more educated about what's right and wrong. And the job didn't appeal to me after that. I sort of drifted away from there. They were more on the "holy" side, and I was having problems with my spiritual life and worked for them. And I guess the mission trip was more of a break from that. I don't guess I've regretted it since. I would like to have had another job somewhere in another line of work. I tried cabinetmaking and at the vo-tech school, and that worked for a couple of years. And you get tired of a place after two years, and here I am at the present time.

Q. You stopped working in 1983?

A. 1983.

Q. It's been two and one-half years since you worked?

A. Yeah, and since Daddy died, we were able to do some deals with the records that he had in the oil industry, which enabled us to get support at this present time. We don't know how long it's going to hold out. That's the reason I'm concerned about the future and how I'm going to support myself.

Q. What was your dad's occupation?

A. Geophysicist.

Q. What was his specialty?

A. Drilling offshore and in marshes.

Q. Wasn't he really well known when he died?

A. Yes, in 1981. And then shortly after that my nephew drowned.

Q. That was P——'s oldest. P——'s only son at that time, right?

A. Yeah.

Q. He had put in a pool and then was supposed to get a fence on next Monday or something.

A. The next day they were getting a fence put around it, and he slipped off and fell in, and I don't know what happened.

Q. How old was he?

A. Two. But at that time, P—— and his wife were expecting. They had another boy. Maybe He allowed it to happen to reach my brothers M—— and P——.

Q. Here's a couple other questions. When you were delivering, or doing your job, did you have any problems in reading maps or finding your way around or any problems with the job? Did you have to do any reading in order to do your job that maybe you couldn't do or could do? Any writing problems?

A. Yeah, the delivery ticket that we got had the address and everything, and you had to deliver it and make sure they got the right stuff. At first, it took me a while to learn.

They had a big map in the office to look at, but then I carried my own map for a while until I got used to places to go. And at first, I would go out and try to locate where I'm going on the map and then figure how to get there. At first, I sort of learned a system to do it, and after a year, then I was secure. I delivered to the stevedores. I didn't know they had several companies so I went to the other stevedores when I should have gone to A—— & D—— Stevedores. And I got the orders mixed up and things like that. It was a problem at first.

Q. That's interesting that you say it was a problem at first and then after you got it down, it worked out. That was a case where you persevered. What made you stick with that and know that it was something you could do? Not something where you would get frustrated like with woodworking that would ultimately make you stop?

A. There was more reading involved and more figuring involved in woodworking where in my delivering all I had to do was worry about the address and the right orders, the merchandise.

Q. Was that a union job?

A. No. I was trying. I filled out applications with other, regular trucking companies, and I never got to that point. I think there was more reading in that kind of driving than what I was doing with M—— Trucking or a private company. They sort of hired anybody off the street, and I guess they were more lenient with me.

Q. Just a question about people that you worked with. Did you get along okay?

A. At first I did. But then after you get used to somebody, you sort of get tired of the way they do things. They were friendly at the beginning, but then after you got to know them, they really weren't anymore. It was more of a cover-up, more of a boss, sort of an authority over you, you have to do what I say.

Q. How about the other truck drivers? Were they okay? Did you get along with them all right?

A. Oh yeah, if you stayed clear of them. Some of them you

got along with and some you didn't get along with. The only way to get along with them is get out on the road and get away from them.

Q. So there wasn't any real togetherness with a group of guys together?

A. They, well, I guess they were in their own world. They liked the girls and the gambling and all the drinking and all that stuff. And I didn't care for that. I mainly stayed to myself, you know. Did my job and stayed away from those situations. They're always in debt and needing money, and I had all my money, but they gambled all theirs away. I think what they do is play cards at lunch and lose it all, and by the time payday comes, they didn't have anything. Of course, with that attitude, they got colorful sometimes.

Q. If you were your own boss, how would you rate your performance? How would you say that you were, on a one to ten scale? Would you say that you were a ten, did very well at your job, or one, meaning you did a very bad job?

A. Somewhere near ten. So real good. I did a real good job.

Q. Were the people that you worked with, the other drivers and your bosses, aware that you were learning disabled?

A. No. I didn't feel it was important to let them know. I filled out my application at the meeting at the job service and through their testing they said . . . I guess they evaluated me as a laborer.

Q. Did they help you find the job? When you went to the job service?

A. I guess after a while they did.

Q. Did they help you find that job at the trucking company?

A. Yeah, I guess.

Q. You told us about some of your educational background. Let me ask. How do you feel that your education has affected you as an adult? Do you feel that there were a lot of things that you learned in school that helped you as an adult?

A. It helped my abilities in reading and taking things slow and studying. I read a lot by myself. I got to a point where instruction, somebody else's instructions, confuses me more than if I sit down and read it myself. Sometimes they put a little too much, too much faster than I'm able to comprehend.

Q. You obviously deal with some reading because you do your Bible studies. Can you tell me about some of the reading that you do?

A. In my Bible?

Q. Well, in your Bible study or other than your Bible study. Are there other things that you read for pleasure?

A. I don't, I don't find books a pleasure. They don't hold my interest. The only thing that's held my interest is the Bible. It's about the future and the past and the present where it holds my interest about things like that. And it's truthful and God's word and nobody else's where it's true, true blue. It's for our best interest.

Q. Do you read any books about commentaries on the Bible?

A. I tried to read other people's books about it. I'm going to a Bible course now at the M— Bible Institute and it's correspondence. I find I do better with correspondence courses because I'm able to go at my own pace, and it's helped me. Other than that, I don't find other people's materials interesting. The M— Bible course was interesting because it related to the Bible more than, it was more of a course than somebody thought. How to read the Bible is easy. I read it like a storybook or a novel. I don't know if I get tired of reading or just get tired.

Q. What are some of the reading problems that you still experience?

A. Comprehension, and I have to read things over and over again what they try to put across. And I can read something and couldn't tell you what I read. At the time I'm reading, I know what I'm reading, but after I've read for a while, I couldn't tell you what I'd read. I guess that's my problem with instructions. Someone tells me something, and I couldn't tell you what they said.

Q. So whether you read it or heard it, it would be about the same? Just comprehension period, whether it's reading or listening?

A. I guess that's my uneasiness about people. They tell me their

name or something like that, you could call it amnesia or
something. It's not that I'm not interested in what they're
saying, just when it gets from here to my thoughts in remembering, I have a problem remembering things. I remember activities, you know, things, actions as far as
communication, somebody is telling you, goes in one ear
and out the other.

Q. How about your math skills? What would you say is about
the most difficult kinds of math you can do or you feel
comfortable with?

A. I can balance my checkbook, but I wouldn't count on it for
higher mathematical.

Q. Can you do percentages?

A. No.

Q. Can you use a calculator pretty well?

A. Yeah, pretty well. I don't know how to punch it out, like
percentages.

Q. Addition, subtraction, how about fractions?

A. I have trouble with fractions.

Q. And division, dividing?

A. Well, dividing not too much with a calculator, it's mainly
percentages and stuff.

Q. You'd rather use a calculator than do it by hand?

A. Yeah.

Q. So, therefore, if you had a job that required some sort of
math, you probably wouldn't feel any more comfortable than
just doing addition, subtraction, multiplication, division on
the calculator, and beyond that you'd feel a little uncomfortable with that?

A. A lot uncomfortable. (Laugh)

Q. I'd like to, somewhat quickly, go through your educational
background. Did you start off in kindergarten?

A. Yes.

Q. And where was that?

A. Kindergarten, I can't remember, it was near L—— School.
I can't think, somewhere in the neighborhood.

Q. Was it in the uptown section of the city?

A. I went to some place where I busted my mouth. (Laughing)
I was running. I guess I was four or five, I guess.

Q. Well, you lived in Orleans Parish, right?

A. Yeah. It was near L—— School. It was in the same area between Carollton and Washington and Napoleon Streets. It was a little neighborhood thing. We used to live on C——. Preschool, or kindergarten, then after that I started to L—— School. I think they start off slow in the first grade, and they didn't know anything about it so then they sent me to S—— School.

Q. What grade did you start S—— School?

A. I guess about second grade.

Q. Private school?

A. Yes, it was on a ways from our house. And then from that I went to second grade, from first to second grade, second to third and fourth grade in mid-city. And from that I went, we moved out here, and I went to, they sent me to J—— A—— School further away from my house. But then they found out about the clinic in B——.

Q. Were you about fourteen then, sixteen?

A. Yeah, and between S——School and M—— C—— and J—— A—— School, they sent me all over the country to different doctors and did physical education on me. And in a school near here, they did the hand-eye coordination.

Q. W—— School?

A. Yeah. I went there.

Q. How long were you at W—— School?

A. I guess just a year.

Q. I was going to ask you what you thought about that.

A. They had me crawl around. That was more than I could take. Then they sent me to a place in San Antonio, to a doctor there. That's when they started me with that. I didn't mind doing it (crawling) there. But then they made me do it here (at home) too, and then my brother's friends would come by, and they would bring their girl friends and all of them would see me doing that (crawling).

Q. Was that kind of a low point for you?

A. It was like I had to go back, I guess I felt like I was failed back to childhood.

Q. Is that right?

A. You know, it's like going to college and saying you have to go back to first grade, you know.

Q. What was your best school experience?

A. When I was in B—— clinic.

Q. Did you live there?

A. Yes. I was an inpatient there. Not inpatient but just a live-in student.

Q. At that time when you were at that school, did they have counseling there as part of their services? Did you talk to counselors every day or social workers?

A. They had doctors, they had counselors that did things with you. You were able to talk to them. They had teachers that were concerned and the director which I was real close to and talked directly to her about problems and ideas and imagination and things like that. We had psychologists like Dr. B——, friends or close friends or acquaintances. They test you about every six months, or every time you sneeze, they check you out. Did EEGs and all that stuff, medication.

Q. And why did you leave?

A. I graduated, well I suppose I graduated.

Q. Graduated from their program at what age?

A. Seventeen.

Q. So that was your last educational experience?

A. Yeah.

Q. Did you get a diploma?

A. Yeah, we got a diploma, and I originally found out that it was an eighth grade diploma, not for twelve years, which I thought it was.

Q. It was more of a certificate of completion?

A. I thought it was, all this time I thought I finished high school you know, but nobody really sat down and told me that it was half way, and I insisted going more, you know.

Q. Did you ever entertain the thought of trying to get your GED?

A. Well, they talked to me about it, you know, but I didn't understand how to go about it.

Q. If someone told you how to go about doing it, two questions. Would you be interested in doing it, and secondly, do you think it would help you? In what ways do you think it would help you if you get your GED, which is the equivalent of graduating from high school?

A. If I had the opportunity, if the right people would help me,

if they offered it. I thought since I had a diploma, I didn't
need it. That is what a GED is, you know, a diploma of
graduation. I have a diploma from A—— S—— correspondence course, and I figured that was sufficient, you know,
there's some more that I need, and I'd be willing to do it.

Q. You may still want to look into that now that you've found
out exactly what your diplomas mean. If you think that it
will help you give you more skills or help you find a job,
you may find that it's worthwhile. But you know that's an
interesting point where you find out many years later that
you don't have what you thought you had. How did you
find out about the worth of your diploma?

A. Mother told me. Until recently, I thought that was it, you
know. Then I went and they tested me at the J—— Vo-Tech
with the California Achievement Test. I think they tested
me at seventh grade or eighth grade, and I had to go back
and retake the test because the first time, I got fourth grade
and had to take the test several times to get up to where I
could get into the course. And the woodworking was the
lowest grade you could get on the course. And if you went
into nursing or cooking, you had to have a twelve for nursing
and a ten for cooking. Judge by that. Since I left high school,
I guess I was more relaxed so I didn't keep up and studied.
If I went a few more years even after I'd graduated, I'd
learn more.

Q. One last question in this area. Let's just say that there was
a magic potion that you could drink, or somebody could
reach in there and connect the wires. What would you like
to be able to do? Like the kinds of skills you would like to
have. What kinds of things would you really wish that you
were able to do?

A. I'd like to write real good like a writer or more ability to
make something of yourself. Accomplish what you want to,
math skills or reading skills and accomplish them.

Q. Would that be the main things?

A. Yeah. You bet.

Q. I have a very simple question. You finished at B——, and
you did some training at D—— in their vocational program,
and you got some training at J—— Vo-Tech too. Since that

time, besides J—— Vo-Tech, have you been involved in any other kind of either vocational education or any counseling or any kind of services?

A. Nothing on a physical labor. But other than seeking training and Spanish-language and Bible training for spiritual work or ministry, somewhere the ministry field, or some kind of physical ministry. At this time I train like that. We'd go to France sometimes and Costa Rica, which involves Spanish and French and their cultures, and learn enough to make my way to there to minister in their language.

Q. Have you taken Spanish courses here?

A. I've taken like Spanish courses. I haven't taken none at school yet but mainly Spanish lessons. I've done it through visual tapes. I don't know what you call it, VCR cassettes.

Q. Just a couple of questions about your daily living routine. We know you like to cook and that your mom typically cooks the meals. If she is out of town, can you cook at home or do you go out and eat? Do you feel confident about making sandwiches, making hot meals, etc., for yourself?

A. I mainly right now do all the cooking. Make the hot chili. I guess you call what I do is amateur gourmet, you know, experiment with different recipes.

Q. Do you follow recipes, directions for recipes?

A. Yeah I do. We ordered this McCall's Cooking School materials. It was like a course, and they send you recipes that you can try and do that way. Each month they sent you another set of recipes like a whole meal and entrées and prepared that from desserts to entrées and different appetizers, and I enjoyed that.

Q. Do you do the food shopping?

A. Sometimes. A little more for her budget, you know, I go for the gourmet type stuff, and she goes for the basics. Cereal and stuff like that. If I spend money for food, might as well make it exciting.

Q. You said that you keep your own checkbook. Are you involved with your mother in money management?

A. When I do the shopping, I use my money. When she does the shopping, she uses her money. She pays the utility bills

and keeps the yard and when things need repair, I try to
do it. If my biorhythm is up, I do it. If not, I don't.

Q. Let me give you a list of things to respond to. I was wondering if you have ever had problems with being on time
for appointments. Do you have problems following directions, or if you have to give directions, is that a problem
for you?

A. Yeah. When I have to give directions, it takes me a while
to get oriented, and I don't know if I'm getting it across
when I try to tell somebody. I guess I mainly have to do it
on paper, show them that way. What was that other
question?

Q. Do you ever have problems with being on time or keeping
track of time?

A. Yes. I have to compensate by being there early for whatever
I do. If I have a doctor's appointment, I try to get there
half an hour earlier to make allowances.

Q. Does that work for you? Always giving yourself extra time?

A. Yeah. When we have Bible studies, I try to be there, it's
7:30. I try to be on the way at 7:00 to make allowances to
get there. Some of them, they can leave almost on time,
five minutes, and be there on time in case I run into
problems.

Q. How close are you to your church?

A. Not far, near C—— Street. There's a 7-11 store, the next
corner is the church, across the street, that's not too far. If
they have like a meeting somewhere, or somewhere else besides the church, I leave early to be on time. I try to experiment, so I try to be there, leave about on time but I'm
always late. I try to get there early.

Q. How's your driving record?

A. Since I've started driving, (laugh) I've had a few mishaps,
(laugh) bump somebody on the rear end.

Q. Reading street signs, is that tough or driving on the interstate? Is that a problem?

A. I usually know where I'm going. If I'm in a strange place,
it takes a while, like we were having problems delivering
when I was trying to find Reverse instead of Reserve (Louisi-

ana). Leaving Reverse, you know, Dairyville or Grayville, LaPlace or places like that, you get worse, and you then call them on the radio and ask them.

Q. You mean on a CB?

A. Well, they had a radio, a business band radio, and were able to talk back to the shop.

Q. I guess that helped a lot?

A. Yeah. I'm leaving Reserve, in Reverse, you know, (laugh) near Grayville, where's Grayville, Dairyville. It was humorous for a while.

Q. I'd like to wrap this interview up with some general questions. You told us a lot about ways that you cope or even overcome some of the problems that you have as you present them. Now I'd like to ask what you think has worked for you? How do you overcome a lot of your problems? Do you see any specific things that you've done?

A. I'm able to get around, able to go across country, around the world, how to make provisions, ways I could handle it for my handicap. So I am able to accomplish going around the world in spite of my problem.

Q. You said sometimes when you were driving the truck, you developed a system for yourself, and you said that you made some provisions for yourself. Can you give me some specific ways that you make these provisions for yourself?

A. Allowing ample time to get there and make, looking at a map before I go there. To mark out my route the way I'm going and go that route. Straight lines, you know, and then after a while, I got used to the route, and then it wasn't a problem for that. Certain places I was able to go right through it. I had problems checking merchandise when I went to pick something up. I was always fearful that I wouldn't miscount or read it wrong. Or sometimes I'd have the wrong order or wrong amount and had to go back and straighten it out.

Q. It does seem that you've learned to cope with a lot of things and ways of getting around. Where do you see the problems you have as a result of learning disabilities? How do they affect you the most now?

A. In getting it right. When fellas tell me once, if I can understand what they said. And fear of getting instructions wrong. Sometimes they tell you real quick, and you've got to remember numbers, phone numbers or addresses, and have to write everything down. Not all the time you have a pencil and paper to write it down. Sometimes things are difficult to spell.

Q. What are some of your goals or hopes for your future?

A. Hope to learn to support myself even if the (inaudible) plays out on me. Support myself, and if I ever got a family, support them and make me a name for myself, contribute something to society, I guess, to life, to contribute to life.

Q. I'm moving from one question to the other right now. We are about finished. It may seem like a peculiar question, but I'm going to ask it anyway. We talked a lot about this thing called learning disabilities, and you can look in books and there are definitions although they may vary from one book to the other. How would you describe or define learning disabilities or what it means to you?

A. In visual way, you reverse words and numbers and remember. So you take a mirror and through the mirror write your name, or write something or trace something, looking through the mirror at what you're doing and that's how it is to reverse words, and when you write something, it's backward, it's opposite of what you're seeing. It's reversing things, if you can imagine writing things backward.

Q. So at times it seems like you are seeing through a mirror, you have to sort it all out?

A. When you see things through a television camera, you see things upside down and backward, but when you see it, it is right side up. (Pause in description) It's reversing letters, I'm drawing a blank now.

Q. You're giving a real, real clear picture. Your descriptions mean a lot more than a definition in a book where they give examples with math and reading or whatever.

A. I have a camera back there. They have a viewfinder, and it's always, it has a reverse mirror in it to straighten the picture out where you can see it. But if you look at the screen itself, it's reversed, it's backward, like when you look through a mirror you turn to see it better. That's like a learning disability or problems with visual perception.

Q. For me that means a lot that you describe it that way. It's a clear picture.

A. I could show a diagram for illustrations. You know mirrors and stuff. They had somebody on, I don't remember who he was, but they were discussing learning disabilities on illustrations on Johnny Carson. Look through the mirror and draw the line and stay within the lines, and he couldn't, sort of do the opposite of what you were seeing. That's what I see when I'm trying to read reversed letters, that was part of it. Expressing myself and visual perception is part of it. That's why I'm slow in school; or I'm slow in reading until you get up in front of class and read a page or something like that, it takes forever. That's where I got self-conscious about doing anything in public, you know, standing up and reading. I start stuttering and stammering.

Q. Have you stood up and talked in front of your Bible class? Do you feel comfortable about doing that? Did you ever do it?

A. If I'm comfortable with the part of the Bible. If I could project myself, I could, but if I had to read it, it would be uncomfortable. I try to get my ideas down where they could understand it. Now in singing and performing, I've played drums publicly at dances and stuff like that and . . .

Q. When was the last time you did that?

A. I guess about two years ago.

Q. You haven't done it since?

A. Now, I try to sing in the choir. It has a lot to do with my self-satisfaction. Something I was able to do and a little more practice could do it some more. But part of the music is something I could project and be able to. I felt like I was offering something. On the Word you know, to contribute to whatever.

Q. I don't have any more questions. You sure have given us a lot of information.

A. I think it's something you all could use.

Q. Oh, absolutely. I think you have done a marvelous job, and

I think you should be very proud. You've given us a lot of insight into a lot of parts about your life, and more importantly, there will be numerous people, especially other adults with learning disabilities, who will be able to relate to and learn a lot from your interview.

A. I hope you can use it.

Q. It will be most useful.

A. What they were doing, they thought was right. I should have had it done earlier and more often or continue until today, continue training, kept after it, kept it going.

Q. Do you think there should have been a more formal transition period?

A. After I got out of school, yes. If I came out and got some kind of training program for working. Because I'm not college material and probably will never be. And if they had some kind of like, correspondence, vocational program where they could train me to be a carpenter or while my mind was still fresh with what they taught you. And whether it be carpentry or mechanics or whatever, you could learn to support yourself.

Q. Why can't that be a goal for the future, now?

A. To continue on with education. I tried before, but I don't have that drive anymore like they drove me.

Q. Any more to add?

A. No, we could probably go on forever. But we can stop now.

Q. Thanks very much.

References

Abbott, R., and Frank, B. 1975. "A Follow-up of LD Children in a Special Private School." *Academic Therapy* 10:291–98.

Balow, B., and Bloomquist, M. 1965. "Young Adults Ten to Fifteen Years after Severe Reading Disability." *Elementary School Journal* 66:44-48.

Blalock, J. 1981. "Persistent Problems and Concerns of Young Adults with Learning Disabilities." In *Bridges to Tomorrow,* edited by W. Cruickshank and A. Silver, 2:3–56. Syracuse, N.Y.: Syracuse University Press.

Buchanan, M., and Wolf, J. 1986. "A Comprehensive Study of Learning Disabled Adults." *Journal of Learning Disabilities* 19:34–38.

Fafard, M., and Haubrich, P. 1981. "Vocational and Social Adjustment of Learning Disabled Young Adults: A Follow-up Study." *Learning Disabilities Quarterly* 4:122–30.

Fitzsimmons, S.; Cheever, J.; Leonard, E.; and Macunovich, D. 1969. "School Failures: Now and Tomorrow." *Developmental Psychology* 1:131–46.

Frauenheim, J. 1978. "Academic Achievement Characteristics of Adult Males Who Were Diagnosed as Dyslexic in Childhood." *Journal of Learning Disabilities* 11:21–28.

Frauenheim, J., and Heckerl, J. 1983. "Longitudinal Study of Psychological Achievement Test Performance in Severe Dyslexic Adults." *Journal of Learning Disabilities* 16:339–47.

Gerber, P. 1981. "Learning Disabilities and Eligibility for Vocational Rehabilitation Services: A Chronology of Events. *Learning Disabilities Quarterly* 4:422–25.

———. 1984. *A Study of the School to Work Transition for Learning Disabled Students and the Learning Disabled Adult in the Netherlands and Denmark*. New York: World Rehabilitation Fund.

———. 1985. "Learning Disabled Students' Transition from School to Work in the Netherlands and Denmark." *Rehabilitation World* 9:12–25.

———. 1986. "The Learning Disabled Adult Nexus: European Perspectives and Emerging American Trends." *Journal of Learning Disabilities* 19:2–4.

Gerber, P. J.; Ginsberg, R.; and Reiff, H. B. 1990. "Identifying Alterable Patterns in Employment Success for Highly Successful Adults with Learning Disabilities." Final Report of grant number H133G80500, National Institute for Disability Research and Rehabilitation, Office of Special Education and Rehabilitative Services, United States Department of Education.

Gerber, P., and Mellard, D. 1985. "Rehabilitation of Learning Disabled Adults: Recommended Research Priorities." *Journal of Rehabilitation* 51:62–64.

Goertz, J., and LeCompte, M. 1984. *Ethnography and Qualitative Design in Educational Research*. New York: Academic Press.

Goyette, A., and Nardini, B. 1985. "The Learning Disabled: A Longitudinal Study of the Transition from School to Work." *Rehabilitation World* 9:27–28.

Hanson, N. 1958. *Patterns of Discovery*. Cambridge: Cambridge University Press.

Hardy, M. 1968. "Clinical Follow-up Study of Disabled Readers." Ph.D., University of Toronto, Canada.

Hinton, G., and Knights, R. 1971. "Children with Learning Problems: Academic History, Academic Prediction, and Adjustment Three Years after Assessment." *Exceptional Children* 37:513–19.

Horn, W.; O'Donnell, J.; and Vitulano, L. 1983. "Long-term Follow-up Studies of Learning Disabled Persons." *Journal of Learning Disabilities* 16:542–55.

Huessy, J., and Cohen, A. 1976. "Hyperkinetic Behaviors and Learning Disabilities Followed over Seven Years." *Pediatrics* 57:4–10.

Hunter, E., and Lewis, H. 1973. "The Dyslexic Child—Two Years Later." *Journal of Psychology* 83:163–70.

Lincoln, Y., and Guba, E. 1985. *Naturalistic Inquiry*. Beverly Hills, Calif.: Sage Publications.

Menkes, M.; Rowe, J.; and Menkes, J. 1967. "A Twenty-five Year Follow-up Study on the Hyperkinetic Child with Minimal Brain Dysfunction." *Pediatrics* 38:393–99.

Miles, M., and Huberman, A. 1984. *Qualitative Data Analysis*. Beverly Hills, Calif.: Sage Publications.

Rawson, M. 1968. *Developmental Language Disability: Adult Accomplishments of Dyslexic Boys*. Baltimore, Md.: Johns Hopkins University Press.

Rogan, L., and Hartman, L. December, 1976. *A Follow-up Study of Learning Disabled Children as Adults*. Final Report. Project #443CH60010, Grant #OEG-0-74-7453. Washington, D.C.: Bureau of Education for the Handicapped, U.S. Department HEW.

Silver, A., and Hagin, R. 1964. "Specific Reading Disability Follow-up Studies." *American Journal of Orthopsychiatry* 24:95–101.

———. 1985. "Outcomes of Learning Disabilities in Adolescence." In *Adolescent Psychiatry: Developmental and Clinical Studies,* edited by M. Sugar, A. Esman, J. Looney, A. Schwartzberg, and A. Sorosky, vol. 12. Chicago: University of Chicago Press.

Spindler, G. 1982. *Doing the Ethnography of Schools.* New York: Holt, Rinehart, and Winston.

Spradley, J. 1979. *The Ethnographic Interview.* New York: Holt, Rinehart, and Winston.

Spreen, O. 1988. "Prognosis of Learning Disability." *Journal of Consulting and Clinical Psychology* 56:836–42.

Weiss, G.; Minde, K.; Werry, J.; Douglas, V.; and Nemeth, E. 1971. "Studies on the Hyperactive Child. Five Year Follow-up." *Archives of General Psychology* 24:409–14.

White, W.; Alley, G.; Deshler, D.; Shumaker, J.; Warner, M.; and Clark, F. 1982. "Are There Learning Disabilities after High School?" *Exceptional Children* 49:273–74.

Will, M. 1984. *OSERS Programming for the Transition of Youth with Disabilities: Bridges from School to Working Life.* Washington, D.C.: United States Department of Education.

Index of Subject Profiles

International Academy for Research in Learning Disabilities Monograph Series

Syracuse University Press

The University of Michigan Press